For Your Information

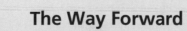

1

Contents

UR 9509329

WX

216

960105

Printed in the UK for the Audit
Commission at Press On Printers, London
ISBN 011 886 4165
London: HMSO

Photographs by Hilary Shedel and with thanks to
Winchester and Eastleigh Healthcare NHS Trust

Preface

The Audit Commission is responsible for the external audit of NHS trusts and other National Health Service bodies in England and Wales. As part of its function the Commission is charged with reviewing the economy, efficiency and effectiveness of services provided by those bodies. To do so, studies and audits of selected topics are undertaken each year.

This study concerns information management in acute hospitals. It was carried out at various study sites across the country. A list of sites is given in Appendix A. Local audits are now under way and will be carried out in acute units in England and Wales during the next year or so.

This report is aimed at trust boards and directors, both managers and clinicians. It identifies the steps that need to be taken to develop information systems that can support healthcare now and in the future. Many of the general lessons are of use to other types of hospitals. The Audit Commission has recently published a review of patient health records, entitled *Setting the Records Straight*, which complements this report (see Appendix B).

The study on which the report is based was carried out by Paul Durham and Martin Adfield under the general direction of Ken Sneath and Dr Roderick Neame. Dr David Young (Consultant Physician), Heather Strachan (Nurse Advisor) and Paul Everington (PA Consultants) provided additional advice. Kevin Akers and Don Jones assisted with data collection and analysis. The study was supported by an advisory group (Appendix A). The Audit Commission is grateful to all individuals and organisations who assisted with this study. Responsibility for the content and conclusions rests solely with the Audit Commission.

1 Healthcare Information

Around 15 per cent of hospital resources are spent on gathering information. Doctors and nurses, for example, spend up to 25 per cent of their time collecting and using information.

Data are collected during patient care encounters. They are used to support clinical decisions, and to monitor clinical and business performance.

Modern healthcare is increasingly complex, requiring many different professionals to collaborate in the care of a single patient. They require access to some common basic information.

Better management of information improves the quality, effectiveness and efficiency of patient care. Information technology can help to achieve these benefits.

Introduction

1.   Information is one of the most important resources that a hospital holds. Most clinical decisions about a patient's care are based on items of data that have been collected previously, both from the current episode (e.g. letters from the referring GP, results of clinical investigations and reports prepared by other professionals) and from notes relating to previous episodes. Not only is information essential for patient care, it is expensive to collect and process the raw data. In addition to the cost of equipment and salaries for staff to support information technology, about 25 per cent of the time of other staff, such as doctors and nurses, is spent collecting data and using information (Ref. 1-5). This means that about 15 per cent of a hospital's running costs are consumed by information.

2.   Because good information, with its associated technology, is an essential component of the drive to improving patient care, it is unlikely that hospitals will wish to reduce expenditure in this area. But there is plenty of potential to improve on what is obtained from spending on information, as well as the efficiency of its production. This report aims to illustrate that potential and suggest ways of realising it.

3.   The main obstacle to getting better value out of information is that staff seldom understand its value or potential. Their perception will only change if they see benefits arriving from information, and this means that it must be made more appropriate, timely, accurate and usable. Information needs to be actively managed; for all practical purposes this means that it has to be computerised. But computers and information technology (IT) must not be allowed to drive the process of information management, only to serve it. It is vital never to lose sight of what the information is needed for and how the hospital uses it. And, although this report is primarily about acute hospitals, it should not be forgotten that information needs and processing increasingly need to be integrated with primary care and other services.

How hospitals use information

4. Information about patients is gathered in the first instance to support clinical decisions, but it has two further critical functions (Exhibit 1) (Ref. 6). One is to monitor and assure the quality of clinical performance. The other is to evaluate business performance and underpin contract management. Most of the information required for these functions can be derived from data collected during patient care encounters.

Exhibit 1
Three uses of information in hospitals

Information collected to support clinical decisions is also used to help monitor clinical performance and evaluate business performance.

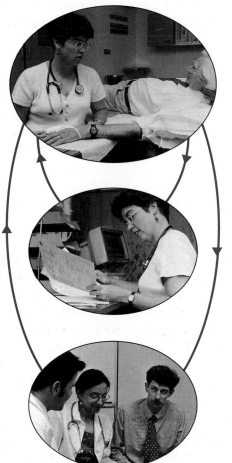

Supporting clinical decisions
- assessing a patient's medical history for relevant problems
- aiding the management of a patient's visit or stay
- assisting with tasks such as producing order forms, discharge letters, etc.
- sharing information about the care and progress of the patient with hospital colleagues, GPs and community care professionals

Monitoring clinical performance
- providing information for audit of individual clinical cases, and for quality assurance relating to services and outcomes
- providing information for research studies into best care practices for specific categories of patients

Evaluating business performance (management, contracting)
- monitoring the quality of care provided, including the achievement of standards of care specified in contracts
- monitoring costs, and taking measures to reduce them where opportunities arise
- ensuring that bills are raised for services provided; comparing costs of care with those at other similar institutions
- making statutory returns to government and international bodies

for your information

A Study of Information Management and Systems in the Acute Hospital

Good information is extremely important to a hospital...

- it is essential for effective patient care, for example in assessing a patient's medical history

- it is used to monitor professional performance and to provide data for research

- it is key to evaluating business and financial performance

... and it is very resource intensive.

- doctors and nurses spend about 25 per cent of their time collecting data and using information

- an average acute hospital spends £8m a year on information (15 per cent of its total costs)

Information needs are changing...

- a patient may be treated by many different staff who all need access to the same information

- others outside the hospital, such as referring GPs, also need access to the information

- public expectations of information are increasing

...and demand good information management.

- to provide better access to clinical information, such as results of investigations

- to produce more accurate administrative and financial information

But investment in information systems has not always delivered the expected benefits...

- systems are often poorly designed or not linked to other systems

- systems procurement and implementation are sometimes haphazard or over-bureaucratic

- staff frequently do not trust the accuracy of the underlying data

- data are often inappropriate for the use for which they are collected

...and there is potential to achieve more within current spending levels.

- by developing plans that are firmly driven by patient needs, not by the technology

- by improving the configuration, procurement and quality of systems

- by standardising and streamlining data collection

- by clearly specifying information needs and investing in data manipulation and analysis skills

Senior management should take the lead by...

- familiarising themselves with the issues involved

- developing a sound information strategy and

- investing in specialist skills and training

..and as a first step they must identify the key information issues in their hospital.

executive briefing

July 1995

A·U·D·I·T COMMISSION

healthcare information

1. Information is one of the most important resources that a hospital holds. Not only is information essential for patient care, it also costs a lot to collect and process. Staff, including doctors and nurses, spend about 25 per cent of their time collecting and using information. Overall the cost of producing information amounts to about 15 per cent of a hospital's running costs, £8 million a year on average.

2. Better information, with its associated technology, is an essential element of achieving better patient care. But there is also potential to achieve considerably more with current spending on information; particularly by ensuring staff receive more appropriate, timely, accurate and usable information.

3. This requires information to be actively managed, which in practical terms means it has to be computerised. But care has to be taken to ensure that the needs of information management drive computers and information technology (IT) and not the other way around.

How hospitals use information

4. The primary purpose of information is to support clinical decisions. It is also used to monitor clinical performance and evaluate business performance (Exhibit 1). But whatever the ultimate use, most of the information has a common origin as data collected during patient care encounters.

Changing information needs

5. Information needs are changing. Modern healthcare is increasingly complex. Large numbers of professionals must collaborate in the care of a single patient - for example a patient with a heart attack may be seen by as many as 25 different staff. They all require access to some common basic information: for example the patient's name, address, GP, results of tests, etc.

6. Not only are there internal needs for the information; much of it has to be made available to others outside the hospital, such as the referring GP or the commissioners of healthcare services. There are also demands for information from research and education. Information systems must keep pace with these growing needs.

7. There are two other important forces for change affecting information requirements and provision:

◆ concerns from all quarters about the security and confidentiality of personal health information held on computer; and

◆ growing public expectations that they will take part in informed decisions about their own care

Benefits from better management of information

8. Good management of information can meet these complex and changing needs. It can also enable the achievement of new levels of quality, effectiveness and efficiency in the delivery of patient care (Exhibit 2, overleaf). This is done by supporting the many tasks, clinical and administrative, involved with delivering care to the patient.

The role of information technology

9. Many of the benefits of information can only be realistically achieved through the use of computers. Computers require data to be well organised and structured, particularly if it is intended to communicate and integrate data between them. Specifically there must be:

◆ semantic standards, which allow meaningful exchange of data from different sources; and

◆ technical standards, which allow dissimilar computers to communicate.

Exhibit 1
Three uses of information in hospitals

Information produced to support clinical decisions is also used to help monitor clinical performance and evaluate business performance.

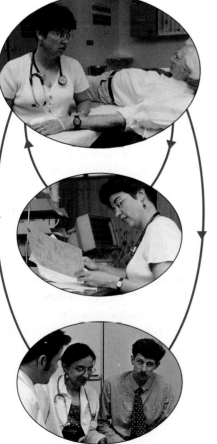

Supporting clinical decisions

● assessing a patient's medical history for relevant problems

● aiding the management of a patient's visit or stay

● assisting with tasks such as producing order forms, discharge letters, etc.

● sharing information about the care and progress of the patient with hospital colleagues, GPs and community care professionals

Monitoring clinical performance

● providing information for audit of individual clinical cases, and for quality assurance relating to services and outcomes

● providing information for research studies into best care practices for specific categories of patients

Evaluating business performance (management, contracting)

● monitoring the quality of care provided, including the achievement of standards of care specified in contracts

● monitoring costs, and taking measures to reduce them where opportunities arise

● ensuring that bills are raised for services provided; comparing costs of care with those at other similar institutions

● making statutory returns to government and international bodies

Exhibit 2
Benefits to patient care from better management of information

Good management of information improves the quality, effectiveness and efficiency of patient care.

Patient process	Benefits	
	Clinical	**Administrative** (some also help clinical staff)
Referral or A&E attendance	Easier access to medical history – past diagnoses – current medication and treatment – drug interactions and allergies	Links to past patient records, saves duplicate data entry Single entry of patient details used across hospital Easier allocation of patient to contract Improved organisation of clinics
Outpatient clinic	Improves location of patient notes Improves access to summary patient details – name, age, GP, etc. – pathology and radiology reports – previous correspondence – discharge letters – clinic letters Easier production of clinic letter to GP Easier access to medical history – past diagnoses – current medication and treatment – drug interactions and allergies	Patient queries quickly dealt with Improved management of waiting lists
Admission	Improves access to summary patient details – name, age, GP, etc. – previous pathology and radiology reports – previous correspondence – discharge letters – clinic letters Supports protocols/guidelines Eases access to results of investigations Quicker reporting of results of therapy	Quicker production of appointment letters Surer location of empty beds More accurate patient details More up-to-date lists of patients admitted Improved planning of ward rounds Easier transfer of patients Improved theatre scheduling
Discharge	Easier discharge planning and documentation Generate discharge summary to GP – discharge diagnosis – relevant history – medication – operation note (if relevant) More reliable data to support clinical audit Shared care better supported with community-based professionals	Easier collection of statistics
Contracting		More accurate billing Enables analysis of activity by GP practice

Source: Audit Commission.

improving the use of health information and IT

10. All hospitals are now computerised to some degree, with administrative and financial systems being the most common. Acquiring and supporting systems currently costs acute hospitals around £220 million a year. Some hospitals spend up to five times as much as others on aquiring and supporting their information systems (Exhibit 3).

11. However, investment in information systems has sometimes failed to deliver benefits to patient care. Problems arise in three main areas:

◆ the collection of data;

◆ the extraction and use of information; and

◆ the quality of the systems themselves.

Data collection

12. There is poor use of information because many staff, especially clinical staff, do not trust the underlying data. They have some justification: for example, in many hospitals more than five per cent of clinical codes are invalid.

13. Despite having to collect data, clinical staff often derive few benefits from using it. Forty per cent of medical staff interviewed by the Audit Commission made little or no use of information reliant on coded clinical data, commonly citing a lack of necessary detail as the reason.

14. If they find the data of little use, clinical staff are unlikely to put much effort into ensuring accuracy,

completeness or timeliness. This is compounded if the purpose of collecting data is not explained.

15. To overcome these problems, hospitals must ensure that all data are collected for a purpose; that information strategy is driven by information needs; and that all staff have the purpose and value of the data explained to them.

Exhibit 3
The cost of acquiring and supporting information systems

Some hospitals spend up to five times as much as others on systems.

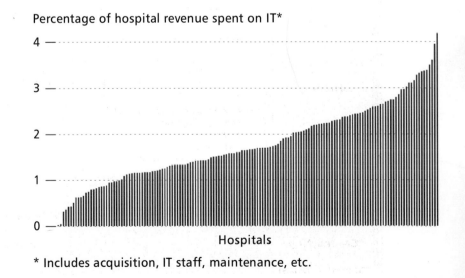

Percentage of hospital revenue spent on IT*

Hospitals

* Includes acquisition, IT staff, maintenance, etc.

Source: Audit Commission analysis of 166 hospitals.

16. Attention must also be given to the sources of data. The focus must be on developing systems that support care and record data about patients at source. The second stage is to link the data to generate robust management and contracting information. In addition, hospitals should:

- ensure data are collected in a form that is clinically useful;

- carry out quality assurance on the data, with clinicians taking a lead responsibility for clinical data and coding; and

- ensure that data capture is made as easy as possible by using available technology.

Using information

17. The purpose of gathering data is to generate useful information on which good decisions can be made. This requires:

- information to be clearly defined by those requesting it;

- investment in skills and software to enable users to generate their own information from systems; and

- employment of expert analysts to extract data, where users cannot be self sufficient.

Systems quality

18. The failure of investment may be to do with the systems themselves. Problems can occur due to:

- poor design of overall systems' configuration, due to a lack of a coherent approach and poor user involvement;

- systems that do not communicate, which as a consequence mean the same data are entered more than once. Most systems are not linked to others (Exhibit 4); in one hospital there were more than 40 separate audit systems, not one of which had links with other systems; and

- out-of-date or badly designed systems that are inflexible, expensive to support and difficult to train staff to use. Nurse care planning systems were viewed to be of doubtful benefit by 70 per cent of nurses interviewed.

Exhibit 4
Computer systems and the extent of linkage

Most systems are not linked to any other systems.

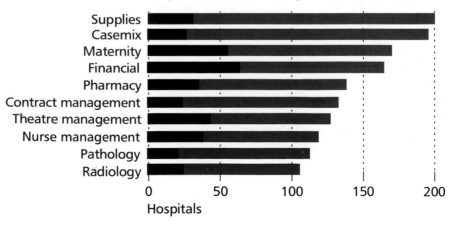

Source: NHS Executive, Information Management Group, HISS survey 1993.

19. In response to these problems hospitals must:

◆ root their information technology plan in their information strategy;

◆ concentrate on developing clinical and operational systems that:

- help with the routine tasks of patient care

- use the patient as a base to grouping information, in order to assist care delivery

- are easy to use

- provide immediate benefits to staff using them

◆ provide links between systems by developing corporate standards.

20. Many of the problems with configuration and quality relate to how the systems were procured and implemented. There are several common problems:

◆ systems' purchasers have poor knowledge about the range of vendors and the systems they offer;

◆ procurement procedures tend to be inflexible and bureaucratic; and

◆ implementation is technology-led, thereby excluding meaningful staff involvement and demotivating staff.

21. A number of measures can help to improve procurement and implementation:

◆ involving users from the very beginning of a project;

◆ creating better access to information on systems and vendors, particularly by better use of external expertise;

◆ ensuring that implementation is led by staff, if possible clinical staff, who understand the core business the system is to serve;

◆ developing formal means of linking procurement to corporate and operational needs for information;

◆ making central guidance more flexible to encourage productive collaboration between systems' purchasers and vendors; and

◆ involving senior management in the whole process and informing them of progress.

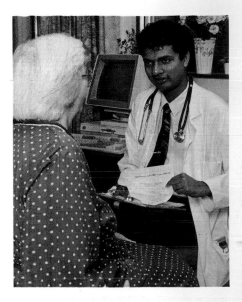

the responsibilities of management

22. Many of the problems mentioned above are perpetuated by senior managers who often neither understand nor 'own' the issues.

Management leadership and commitment

23. In order to make progress trust boards need to break through a vicious circle of poor understanding of information issues by:

♦ educating themselves about health information and technology, for example by visiting good practice sites; and

♦ ensuring proper executive representation at board level of the information function.

Improving planning

24. A trust must have a strategy for information systems and technology that:

♦ is driven by the trust's information needs;

♦ sets data and technical standards to enable a move towards the integration of information;

♦ reviews the options for financing investments; and

♦ learns lessons from previous experiences through formal evaluation and feedback to management.

Investing in staff

25. Trusts have two main challenges in relation to staff. They must ensure that:

♦ they have enough specialist staff with the necessary skills and understanding; and

♦ all staff are equipped to use information and information systems productively through investment in education and training.

Ensuring security and confidentiality of health information

26. Boards must accept responsibility for the security and confidentiality of data by:

♦ ensuring all new systems bought have a full range of access controls, audit trails, etc; and

♦ developing policies and rules that protect personal data.

The way forward

27. As a first step, managers need to know where they are starting and the key issues in their hospital. The full report, of which this is a summary, provides a strengths and weaknesses checklist to start this process.

28. There are also local audits taking place, carried out by auditors appointed by the Audit Commission, which will explore many of the issues in the report.

If you want to know more:

The full details of this Audit Commission study are published in the National Report, *For Your Information: A Study of Information Management and Systems in the Acute Hospital.*

Published by HMSO
ISBN 011 886 416 5
Price £10

Telephone orders 0171 873 9090

The Audit Commission for Local Authorities and the National Health Service in England and Wales, 1 Vincent Square, London SW1P 2PN   Tel: 0171-828 1212

◆ **Monitoring clinical performance** enables staff to ensure that patients receive the best possible care, that care services are of a uniformly high quality and that the outcomes of care are consistent with the best results from elsewhere. There is a requirement, therefore, routinely to audit randomly selected cases, to report on all exceptional cases (e.g. long stays, poor outcomes) and to generate summaries of patients by category and provider. These summaries can be used to monitor outcomes over time or for comparison with established norms (e.g. seeking evidence of excessive post-operative infection rates or unusual proportions of Caesarean sections). To optimise outcomes and minimise costs it is vital to identify ineffective services and circumstances where one therapeutic plan is more likely to be successful than another.

◆ **Evaluating business performance** involves gathering the data required for billing and contract management, keeping a record of services provided and of patients treated and tracking costs incurred in providing care to the relevant patients. It also involves calculating the aggregate costs of providing each service and identifying underutilised staff, equipment and facilities.

Changing information needs

5.   Information needs are not static. As healthcare and information systems both evolve, so do the hospital's information needs. The growing complexity of modern medical care has led to the development of care teams, with large numbers of professionals collaborating in the care of a single individual. A patient with a heart attack, for example, may be seen by as many as 25 professionals during their hospital stay. They all require access to some common basic information: for example, name, address and biographical details, diagnosis, care plans, results of tests and investigations (Exhibit 2, overleaf). Any failure of information systems to keep pace with this growing complexity can be very wasteful. In one hospital in this study basic patient details were sometimes recorded 13 times.

6.   Much hospital information has to be made available to individuals and groups external to the hospital. A summary of an episode of care is normally returned to the referring GP and may also be sent to other community-based service providers. A summary of each case treated by a hospital is returned to the Department of Health or Welsh Office for use in national statistics. And commissioners of healthcare services require detailed analyses of treatment, its cost and its effectiveness, in order to manage their contracts, pay appropriate claims and plan for future commissioning. Increasingly, therefore, hospital information needs to be integrated with information in other parts of the healthcare system.

Exhibit 2
Common needs for information

There are common needs for information amongst the different hospital (and community) staff involved in a patient's care.

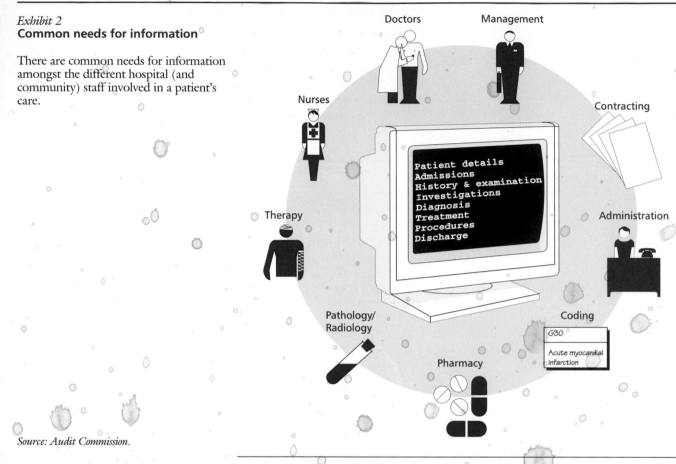

Doctors   Management

Nurses

Contracting

Therapy

Patient details
Admissions
History & examination
Investigations
Diagnosis
Treatment
Procedures
Discharge

Administration

Pathology/
Radiology

Coding

G30

Acute myocardial infarction

Pharmacy

Source: Audit Commission.

7. Information needs are also driven by developments in research and teaching. Routine patient care information is increasingly used for research into the best ways to treat specific conditions. It also forms the foundation for much clinical audit of the effective and efficient application of services. Some hospitals have an additional requirement for information and case studies to support the education of future healthcare professionals.

8. It seems likely that healthcare providers will increasingly invest in information as healthcare becomes more complex and as commissioners start to demand better evidence of the quality and quantity they are getting for their money. Two other forces for change deserve special mention. One is the concern over confidentiality of data held on computer. The other is the growing expectation by the public that they will take part in informed decision making about their own care.

Concerns about security and confidentiality

9. Personal health information is, for the most part, highly sensitive. Without proper controls, information stored in computerised information management systems is much more readily accessible to outsiders than the same information stored in manual filing systems, and linkages between computerised records for the same person can be more easily established (Ref. 7). At the same time patient data are also used for an increasing range of purposes, such as contracting. For these reasons public and practitioner concerns over security and confidentiality issues are on the increase.

10. Practitioners and institutions have always been required to ensure that information kept about an individual is secure, private and confidential. The Hippocratic Oath that guides doctors' ethical behaviour includes the statement: *'Whatever in connection with my professional practice, or not in connection with it, I see or hear, in the life of men, which ought not to be spoken of abroad, I will not divulge, as reckoning that all such should be kept secret.'*

11. In response to these new concerns about computerised data, additional new rules and regulations have been developed. The Data Protection Act covers personal data stored on computers in the UK, and a variety of international initiatives (OECD guidelines, current EC mandates and directives) and local legislation will have major impact on the management of healthcare information (Refs. 8 - 14). All of these necessary initiatives add to the information handling tasks of hospitals.

Growing public expectations

12. Empowerment of patients to take an active role in their own healthcare is recognised as of growing importance by patients and professionals alike. Provision of appropriate information at the right times can ensure that patients are aware of the potential benefits and risks associated with options for their future care. Effective information management can:

- support the individual patient in choosing their treatment, self-management of their condition and assessment of the outcome (Refs. 15 and 16);
- underpin good communication between clinical staff and patients;
- improve medical outcomes through improved patient access to health information (Ref. 17); and
- help meet patients' expectations of confidentiality, integrity and continuity of care across providers.

13. Patients increasingly (and rightly) expect more from the health service. They want to be told what is available, what they can expect and when they can expect it. The Patient's Charter aims to meet some of these expectations (Ref. 18). It sets out rules which aim to ensure that patients receive timely and appropriate care services – with specific time limits set for receiving treatment and with sufficient information to explain the treatment available, together with the risks and alternatives. All of this creates new demands for accurate and timely health information.

Benefits from better management of information

14. These complex and changing needs will only be met if information is well managed. Well-managed information: is based on data that have been validated through day-to-day use; is efficiently stored, processed and retrieved; and is produced in response to a need rather than because the data are available. Moreover, not only does good management of information meet existing uses and changing needs, but it can improve the quality, effectiveness and efficiency of patient care (Exhibit 3):

- Individual care can be better organised and coordinated in a variety of ways. For example, better outpatient scheduling systems can reduce waiting times and improve access (Ref. 19); letters to GPs from outpatient clinics can be generated almost as a side product from good clinical information and empty beds can be located more rapidly and accurately for acutely ill patients.

- Availability of a medical record in several places at once can improve the quality of patient care. For example, the risks of drug interactions and problems from incompatible care plans will be minimised.

- Information can be communicated more quickly and reliably.

- Analysis of patient dependency levels and projection of probable lengths of stay (provided they are done properly) can help ensure the right numbers of staff with appropriate skills are available at the right time in the right place.

- Time consuming and irritating duplicate data entry can be eliminated.

- Hospitals can cost their services more accurately.

- Analysis of workload statistics can identify variation in productivity.

Any improvements in efficiency of clinical staff, driven by such changes, will enable them to spend more time with patients.

The role of information technology

15. Many of the benefits of information can only be realistically achieved through the use of computers. But to use computers, data must be organised and structured. Data stored on computers as 'free text' are no easier to summarise or manipulate than handwritten records in a filing cabinet. However, computer data can be coded uniquely so that they represent a service, drug, illness or investigation. Such information can then be displayed, analysed or combined into reports as the user requires. This facility is essential for many new requirements, such as costing, contract management and audit.

Exhibit 3
Benefits to patient care from better management of information

Good management of information improves the quality, effectiveness and efficiency of patient care.

Benefits		
Patient process	**Clinical**	**Administrative** (some also help clinical staff)
Referral or A&E attendance	Easier access to medical history – past diagnoses – current medication and treatment – drug interactions and allergies	Links to past patient records, saves duplicate data entry Single entry of patient details used across hospital Easier allocation of patient to contract Improved organisation of clinics
Outpatient clinic	Improves location of patient notes Improves access to summary patient details – name, age, GP, etc. – pathology and radiology reports – previous correspondence – discharge letters – clinic letters Easier production of clinic letter to GP Easier access to medical history – past diagnoses – current medication and treatment – drug interactions and allergies	Patient queries quickly dealt with Improved management of waiting lists
Admission	Improves access to summary patient details – name, age, GP, etc. – previous pathology and radiology reports – previous correspondence – discharge letters – clinic letters Supports protocols/guidelines Eases access to results of investigations Quicker reporting of results of therapy	Quicker production of appointment letters Surer location of empty beds More accurate patient details More up-to-date lists of patients admitted Improved planning of ward rounds Easier transfer of patients Improved theatre scheduling
Discharge	Easier discharge planning and documentation Generate discharge summary to GP – discharge diagnosis – relevant history – medication – operation note (if relevant) More reliable data to support clinical audit Shared care better supported with community-based professionals	Easier collection of statistics
Contracting		More accurate billing Enables analysis of activity by GP practice

Source: Audit Commission.

16. However, there is no guarantee that even data which are well organised and structured can be freely communicated and integrated with other information. Linking dissimilar computer systems and sources of information will require a degree of discipline and expenditure that may not give any immediate return. Nevertheless, the significant gains which are possible from health information management will only come about if systems are integrated. This will mean adoption of, and adherence to, certain agreed standards. There are two groups of standards that matter: *technical standards*, which allow dissimilar computers to communicate; and *semantic standards,* which allow meaningful exchange of data from different sources.

Technical standards

17. Computers all work in different ways, using different operating systems, application software and communications protocols. Agreements are required to enable two computers to be linked together and to work together successfully. These are technical standards. There is no shortage of suitable standards to adopt; however, there is little evidence in most hospitals of a policy on common technical standards and this will make it more difficult to link systems and machines together.

18. In practice, many developers have created devices for linking together technically unlike systems, and so the problem has been solved piecemeal. But, as the number of different systems grows, the cost of linking them will become prohibitive, unless common standards have been adopted (see Box 1). The same principle also applies to the data contained in the systems, which must comply with semantic standards.

Semantic standards

19. The other key group of standards relates to the meaningful exchange of data and creates problems that are much less easy to solve. In order to encapsulate in a concise way information, such as the details of a patient stay or the results of a blood test, there must be agreements as to how to describe the options (so-called 'terming') and how each is to be coded and classified (see Appendix C). All hospitals are required to adopt standard codes, such as the International Classification of Diseases (ICD) for classifying illness and treatment. Others have adopted coding systems such as the Read codes or developed their own coding systems (Ref. 20). Yet others have passively accepted any coding systems that may have been incorporated in the applications they have purchased. The problem comes when a need arises to link systems using different codes – for example, to compare information between hospitals. It is difficult and expensive to map coding systems to each other, especially when many of the systems evolve over time so requiring a new map to be made every time either coding system is updated. Indeed, it may not even be possible. Adoption of standards is one of the few options for 'future-proofing' technology investment.

Box 1
The standards issue

As the number of different systems grows, so does the importance of common standards.

There are two approaches to linking computerised systems: one is based on the use of standards; the other is not.

Each link between two systems, A and B, requires two interfaces (translators), one from A to B and the other from B to A.

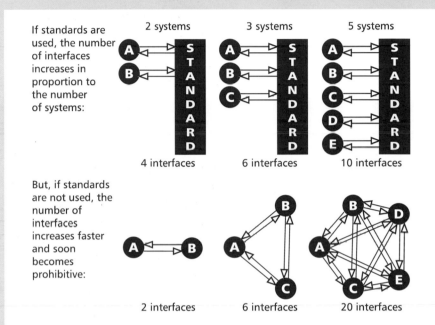

If standards are used, the number of interfaces increases in proportion to the number of systems:

2 systems — 4 interfaces
3 systems — 6 interfaces
5 systems — 10 interfaces

But, if standards are not used, the number of interfaces increases faster and soon becomes prohibitive:

2 interfaces
6 interfaces
20 interfaces

Standards are vital if systems are to communicate. Other advantages are:

◆ they introduce a degree of stability in the environment, promoting investment and confidence;

◆ they offer a level of 'future-proofing' of systems investments; and

◆ they permit fairer competition between suppliers.

Standards bodies

The UK has a national standards body, the British Standards Institute (BSI); Europe has a community standards body, the Comité Européen Normatif (CEN). Sitting above these are several international standards bodies, such as the International Standards Organisation (ISO). These bodies develop, by consensus, formal standards at national, regional and international levels. Additional ad hoc solutions arise out of consumer uptake, government directives and industry pressure groups and are just as important.

20. The Department of Health and Welsh Office lead or take an active role in the development of a range of standards designed for national and international use, for example:

◆ data interchange and medical message exchanges;

◆ open systems and computing environments;

◆ security and data protection;

◆ data sets, classification and coding; and

◆ data standards and definitions.

These standards are intended to form the foundation of a national system for health information management and communication. The Information Management Group (IMG) of the NHS Executive, as part of its brief, disseminates information about standards and promotes their incorporation in procurements.

Conclusion

21. There are significant benefits to be gained from good information management, and computers have an essential part to play in achieving those benefits. While there are important benefits to be gained immediately, the future potential for information backed by good information technology is enormous. Computerised healthcare information will not only support and improve existing healthcare, but will in time enable the nature of the care process itself to change in directions otherwise unimaginable. The combination of computerised information with telecommunications and electronic sensing devices will allow (and already in some countries is allowing) patients to be monitored whilst at home or diagnoses to be made by specialists acting at a distance. And the development of software that allows large amounts of information to be brought to bear on individual decisions (through concepts such as expert systems and decisions support tools) will extend the repertoire of skills of professionals at all levels.

22. Meanwhile in most countries, including the UK, such radical change is a long way off. And there are some problems with the existing investment in health information technology and its yield. The next chapter describes the current state of health information and IT in England and Wales, considers why they have not delivered all the benefits they might and suggests some solutions based on observed good practice.

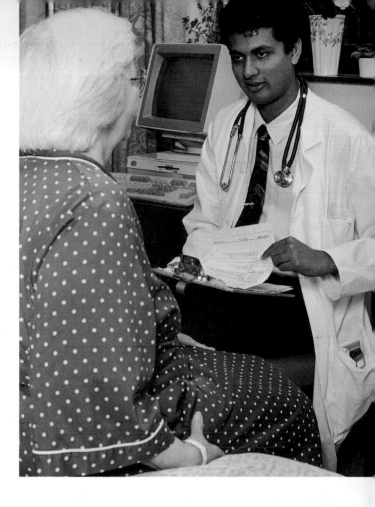

Most hospitals now have computer systems, particularly for administration and finance. Annually £220 million is spent by acute hospitals on systems. However this investment has often failed to benefit patient care.

The data collected are often of poor quality because the clinical staff, who collect them, get little benefit from their use. Data must be collected in a form that is clinically useful and checked before use. Data capture must be made as easy as possible, using technology.

Information can often be improved using currently available data. To achieve this, information requirements should be clarified; and investment made in skills and software.

Many systems are not linked, are inflexible and difficult to use. They must be developed within a wider strategy and be primarily designed to improve the delivery of patient care, rather than support finance and administration. Procurement and development of systems need to be led by users.

2 Improving the Use of Healthcare Information and IT

Introduction

23. Information technology and computers in particular must be central to any initiative to improve the value obtained from health information. Computers have been progressively introduced into acute hospitals in England and Wales since the 1960s, starting with financial systems such as ledgers and payrolls, moving through administrative ones such as patient administration systems (PAS) and more recently into areas such as clinical audit and clinician support. All hospitals are now computerised to some degree, with the older, more administrative and financial systems being the most prevalent (Exhibit 4).

24. Not surprisingly this level of computerisation has required substantial investment, both for the original purchase and installation and for support and maintenance. Acute hospitals in England and Wales currently spend £220m annually on acquiring, installing and supporting systems. This averages around 1.8 per cent of total hospital revenue, a level not dissimilar to hospitals in other European countries, although considerably lower than those in the US where activity is costed in fine detail for insurance purposes. It is considerably lower than many other sectors of the economy – banking or insurance for example (Ref. 21).

25. Some hospitals are much more highly computerised than others. The cost of acquiring and supporting information systems varies at least fivefold when expressed as a percentage of all revenue (Exhibit 5). Part of this variation is due to the effect of central funding. On average 20 per cent of the funds for developing information systems have in the past been provided by the Department of Health and the Welsh Office, but some hospitals received considerably more than others. However, it is now widely acknowledged that much central funding resulted in information systems that did not deliver the expected benefits. The policy on funding has now changed, with the introduction in 1992 of the information management and technology (IM&T) strategy (Ref. 22). This delegates the responsibility for making investment and funding to individual hospitals (Box 2).

Exhibit 4
Current information systems

Administrative and financial systems are the most prevalent.

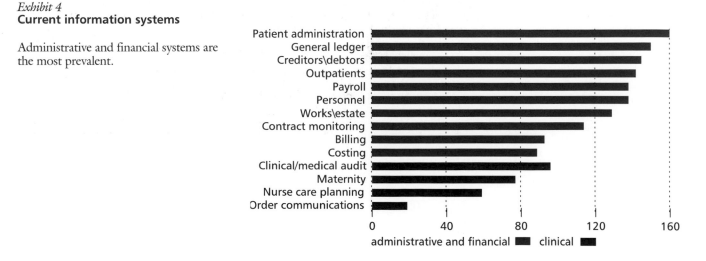

Source: Audit Commission analysis of 166 hospitals.

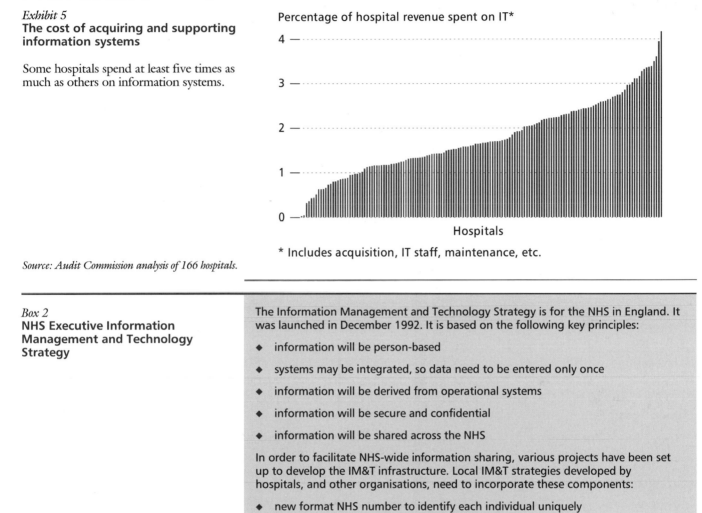

Exhibit 5
The cost of acquiring and supporting information systems

Some hospitals spend at least five times as much as others on information systems.

Percentage of hospital revenue spent on IT*

Hospitals

* Includes acquisition, IT staff, maintenance, etc.

Source: Audit Commission analysis of 166 hospitals.

Box 2
NHS Executive Information Management and Technology Strategy

The Information Management and Technology Strategy is for the NHS in England. It was launched in December 1992. It is based on the following key principles:

- information will be person-based
- systems may be integrated, so data need to be entered only once
- information will be derived from operational systems
- information will be secure and confidential
- information will be shared across the NHS

In order to facilitate NHS-wide information sharing, various projects have been set up to develop the IM&T infrastructure. Local IM&T strategies developed by hospitals, and other organisations, need to incorporate these components:

- new format NHS number to identify each individual uniquely
- shared NHS administrative registers holding patient details
- the availability of a rational thesaurus of coded clinical terms and groupings (Read codes and health resource groups)
- a system of NHS-wide networking to enable information to be shared
- national standards for computer-to-computer communication
- a framework for security and confidentiality

Exhibit 6
Availability of terminals on wards

The number of terminals and personal computers provided on wards varies considerably.

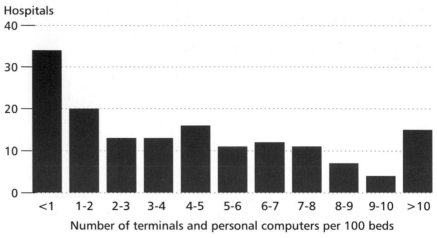

Hospitals

Number of terminals and personal computers per 100 beds

Source: Audit Commission analysis of 166 hospitals.

26. The number of terminals and personal computers provided in wards varies considerably (Exhibit 6). Moreover, access is better for administrative than for clinical staff (Exhibit 7). So it is hardly surprising that half of ward nursing staff and 15 per cent of medical staff interviewed at study sites reported being unable to access systems at peak usage times.

27. Unfortunately, not all investment in IT has been successful. Perhaps the acid test of achievement by IT is whether front-line staff perceive themselves to have benefited from it. In the NHS many do not. The majority of ward nurses interviewed by the Audit Commission doubted that their nursing care planning systems brought any overall benefit. Interviews with doctors and nurses in hospitals visited by the Commission show that clinical staff are no more likely to perceive benefits in hospitals that spend more on IT (Exhibit 8). Some hospitals have achieved valuable benefits in information management with relatively modest IT expenditure, while others have achieved little despite great investment.

28. If investment in IT has sometimes failed to deliver benefits to hospital care, it is important to understand why. Problems arise in three main areas: the collection of data; the extraction and use of information; and the procurement and implementation of information systems.

Data collection

29. One of the main reasons for scepticism and poor use of information is that staff, especially clinical staff, do not trust the data. Around 60 per cent of clinical audit staff interviewed during this study reported problems of inaccurate coding. Half of clerical staff interviewed felt there were significant errors in coding. These perceptions are supported by evidence from several recent studies of data accuracy (Refs. 23 - 26). In many hospitals more than five per cent of clinical codes are invalid (Exhibit 9).

Exhibit 7
Ratios of terminals to staff

Access is better for administrative than for clinical staff.

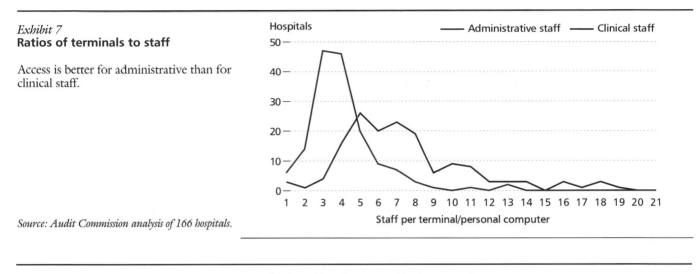

Source: Audit Commission analysis of 166 hospitals.

Exhibit 8
IT expenditure and perceived benefits in acute hospitals

Clinical staff are no more likely to perceive benefits in hospitals that spend more on IT.

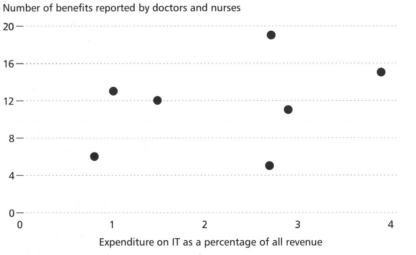

Source: Audit Commission analysis of study sites.

Exhibit 9
The percentage of invalid codes in diagnostic data

In many hospitals more than five per cent of clinical codes are invalid.

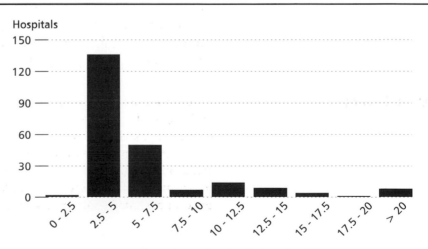

Source: Department of Health and Welsh Office hospital episode statistics 1992/93 and 1993/94.

19

'All too often a decision to collect data is made before thought has been given as to how they will be turned into information'

30. Forty per cent of the medical staff interviewed thought the data abstracts for contract management and for reporting to the Department of Health and the Welsh Office were not recorded in a form that described the clinical case meaningfully – they were criticised either as being insufficiently detailed (where ICD codes and descriptors are used) or inappropriate (where casemix entities such as diagnosis-related groups are used). Consequently they made little or no use of the data.

31. The principal source of data in a hospital is the medical record. In most institutions this remains handwritten on paper and suffers from all the problems of 'static' text. Everything is mixed up together. Abstraction of data is consequently laborious, costly and inaccurate. To make matters worse, the last two decades have seen a rapid growth in non-clinical demand for data abstracts and summaries. Sometimes this is addressed by requiring clinical staff to complete additional forms purely for management and contracting purposes, an unwelcome development that has taken valuable clinical time away from patient care. In other hospitals clerks have been assigned the task of abstracting data from the casenotes, but it has proved difficult to find all the data elements required for completion of the forms in a document as complex, technical and disorganised as the medical record.

32. Administrative and financial computing systems have been developed largely in isolation from clinical information management, relying on the completion of forms for their data inputs. Asking staff to collect large amounts of data is likely to be viewed by them as burdensome, especially if the purpose of collection has not been adequately explained. And even then, unless there is some perceived or tangible benefit to the staff involved, it is unlikely that much effort will be put into ensuring that the data collected are accurate, complete or timely.

33. Whether there is tangible benefit or not will largely depend upon whether the information needs have been clarified first. All too often a decision to collect data is made before thought has been given as to how they will be turned into information, or whether there is a need to collect them at all. Decisions are often based on the availability of data and the ease of collection, rather than on whether or not collecting it would create useful information. As a consequence, it often later becomes apparent that the wrong data have been collected, or that data have been classified in an inappropriate way or using an inappropriate system to meet the reporting needs.

34. To overcome these problems, hospitals must first and foremost ensure that all data are collected for a purpose, and that information strategy is driven by information needs. Development of administrative and financial management systems is unlikely to succeed without sufficient attention to their sources of data. The focus must be on development of operational support systems and particularly on those which record data about patients at source. The second step can then be to link them to feed data to administrative systems. In addition to this, hospitals should:

◆ ensure that data are collected in a form that is clinically meaningful, but at the same time capable of being re-used to generate robust management and contracting information;

◆ carry out some form of quality assurance on data; and

◆ ensure that data capture is as easy as possible for those involved.

Collecting data in the right form

35. Significant effort is needed to collect clinical data in a form that is suitable for re-use, for example, in casemix analysis or activity returns. The Read codes (Box 3, overleaf) are well suited for this purpose; they are designed for clinical staff and use terms that are clinically acceptable and meaningful. Each term is attached to a code and each code is cross-mapped to equivalent codes in other key systems, such as ICD (for diagnostic classification) and OPCS (for procedure classification). Thus, in principle, there is little extra effort involved in producing reports in these formats. However, navigation of the Read codes to find the right specific term in the first place is not a trivial task and is variably addressed by different software applications. Navigation needs to be simplified if the Read codes or some equivalent are to be used more widely in hospitals.

36. Clinical staff are the best placed to collect some items, for example, the data required for casemix analysis and for contract management. This can be addressed by ensuring that individual consultants accept a degree of managerial responsibility for the business success of their clinical unit; its income, growth and continued operation will then become a part of their operational responsibility, and this can be expected to broaden the range of operational data that is valued and validated at source.

37. Persuading consultants to accept responsibility for data collection and coding is not always possible. It must be made acceptably easy, and this may require significant investment in systems and terminals. Many hospitals have, for the time being at least, to delegate the task to supporting clerical and secretarial staff. This increases the risk of error, particularly as the separation between originator and coder increases. In such circumstances it is necessary to have some form of data quality assurance.

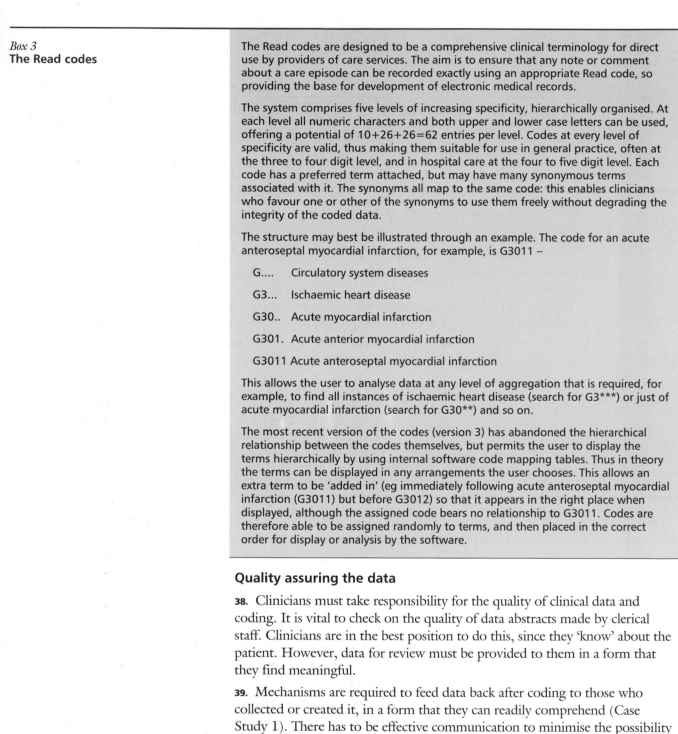

Box 3
The Read codes

The Read codes are designed to be a comprehensive clinical terminology for direct use by providers of care services. The aim is to ensure that any note or comment about a care episode can be recorded exactly using an appropriate Read code, so providing the base for development of electronic medical records.

The system comprises five levels of increasing specificity, hierarchically organised. At each level all numeric characters and both upper and lower case letters can be used, offering a potential of 10+26+26=62 entries per level. Codes at every level of specificity are valid, thus making them suitable for use in general practice, often at the three to four digit level, and in hospital care at the four to five digit level. Each code has a preferred term attached, but may have many synonymous terms associated with it. The synonyms all map to the same code: this enables clinicians who favour one or other of the synonyms to use them freely without degrading the integrity of the coded data.

The structure may best be illustrated through an example. The code for an acute anteroseptal myocardial infarction, for example, is G3011 –

G....   Circulatory system diseases

G3...   Ischaemic heart disease

G30..   Acute myocardial infarction

G301.   Acute anterior myocardial infarction

G3011 Acute anteroseptal myocardial infarction

This allows the user to analyse data at any level of aggregation that is required, for example, to find all instances of ischaemic heart disease (search for G3***) or just of acute myocardial infarction (search for G30**) and so on.

The most recent version of the codes (version 3) has abandoned the hierarchical relationship between the codes themselves, but permits the user to display the terms hierarchically by using internal software code mapping tables. Thus in theory the terms can be displayed in any arrangements the user chooses. This allows an extra term to be 'added in' (eg immediately following acute anteroseptal myocardial infarction (G3011) but before G3012) so that it appears in the right place when displayed, although the assigned code bears no relationship to G3011. Codes are therefore able to be assigned randomly to terms, and then placed in the correct order for display or analysis by the software.

Quality assuring the data

38. Clinicians must take responsibility for the quality of clinical data and coding. It is vital to check on the quality of data abstracts made by clerical staff. Clinicians are in the best position to do this, since they 'know' about the patient. However, data for review must be provided to them in a form that they find meaningful.

39. Mechanisms are required to feed data back after coding to those who collected or created it, in a form that they can readily comprehend (Case Study 1). There has to be effective communication to minimise the possibility of errors (Ref. 23). For example, where a term has been used that is ambiguous or unclear to the coder, there must be a means of checking what was intended by this use of terminology. This communication is facilitated where coders work for specific clinical directorates and know the clinical staff. To support a closer working relationship, coders should be in regular contact with those staff whose work they code. At the same time there must be consistency of coding across the entire hospital.

Case Study 1
Quality control of medical coding

Ipswich Hospital NHS Trust

In a large general hospital of about 900 beds each clinician is invited to spend time with clinical coders to discuss the coding of twenty episodes of care. This is then compared to the consultant's opinion as to what diagnoses and procedures should have been coded from the clinical notes. On average there is agreement on 85 per cent of the codes. Where there are problems, either the coder's process of extracting codes from the notes is changed or the clinicians change their practice of note taking. There is also a discussion of the general problems coders have faced interpreting the clinical notes and converting them into codes.

This two-way contact helps coder and clinician to understand each other better. Some consultants now offer coders the chance to attend clinical lectures.

Simplifying data capture

40. It is necessary to make data entry as convenient as possible for those responsible. Priority must be given to ease-of-use (Ref. 27). Technologies such as bar code readers, optical mark readers or point and click devices can be selectively exploited to minimise the effort of inputting some types of data such as patient identifiers. Portable or hand-held devices can reduce the duplicate recording of data on paper and computer. And, at a basic level, provision of sufficient terminals in appropriate locations to meet peak workloads is essential if usage is to be encouraged.

Using information

41. The purpose of gathering data is to generate useful information on which good decisions can be made. If the data quality is dubious, potential users will boycott the information. But even if the data quality is good, the information may still not be used as effectively as it could.

42. There are various possible explanations:

◆ the decision maker may not be clear what information would be useful in making a particular decision, or the person responsible for its extraction may not have fully understood what was required;

◆ the availability or location of the necessary data may be unknown to the analyst (e.g. held on a departmental stand-alone microcomputer) or they may be held in a form or on a system that cannot readily be accessed or used;

◆ when relevant and accurate information is prepared, it, nevertheless, may not be in a form that is readily comprehended, or may contain too much distracting detail, and the essential messages may be lost or diluted as a consequence; or

◆ the information may not be available in time to affect decisions that have to be made. Half of chief executives and board members interviewed believed financial information was not sufficiently up to date. One reason might be that in many hospitals only 40 per cent of coding was completed within four weeks of discharge (Ref. 26). This meant information on income was difficult to equate with expenditure.

Case Study 2
Information manager

Addenbrooke's NHS Trust, Cambridge.

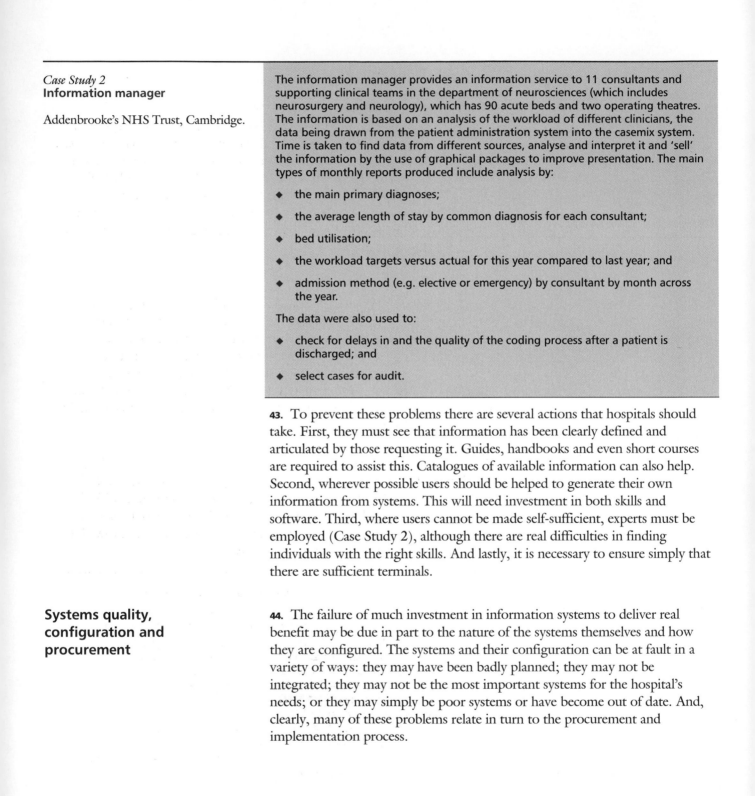

The information manager provides an information service to 11 consultants and supporting clinical teams in the department of neurosciences (which includes neurosurgery and neurology), which has 90 acute beds and two operating theatres. The information is based on an analysis of the workload of different clinicians, the data being drawn from the patient administration system into the casemix system. Time is taken to find data from different sources, analyse and interpret it and 'sell' the information by the use of graphical packages to improve presentation. The main types of monthly reports produced include analysis by:

◆ the main primary diagnoses;

◆ the average length of stay by common diagnosis for each consultant;

◆ bed utilisation;

◆ the workload targets versus actual for this year compared to last year; and

◆ admission method (e.g. elective or emergency) by consultant by month across the year.

The data were also used to:

◆ check for delays in and the quality of the coding process after a patient is discharged; and

◆ select cases for audit.

43. To prevent these problems there are several actions that hospitals should take. First, they must see that information has been clearly defined and articulated by those requesting it. Guides, handbooks and even short courses are required to assist this. Catalogues of available information can also help. Second, wherever possible users should be helped to generate their own information from systems. This will need investment in both skills and software. Third, where users cannot be made self-sufficient, experts must be employed (Case Study 2), although there are real difficulties in finding individuals with the right skills. And lastly, it is necessary to ensure simply that there are sufficient terminals.

Systems quality, configuration and procurement

44. The failure of much investment in information systems to deliver real benefit may be due in part to the nature of the systems themselves and how they are configured. The systems and their configuration can be at fault in a variety of ways: they may have been badly planned; they may not be integrated; they may not be the most important systems for the hospital's needs; or they may simply be poor systems or have become out of date. And, clearly, many of these problems relate in turn to the procurement and implementation process.

'There has been a bias towards administrative and financial systems'

System configuration and quality

Poor design of the systems configuration

45. The lack of any coherent information strategy within many hospitals has resulted in a piecemeal approach to development. And failure to involve users, especially clinical professionals, has meant that commitment is lost and that they have sometimes been forced to express their individuality and acquire or develop their own applications. The result is confusion: for example, a mainframe HIS system together with one or many microcomputer systems serving key functions, such as audit or directorate management, but with no connection between them.

Systems that do not communicate

46. Most systems, even those with patient administration details, are not linked to any other systems (Exhibit 10). This is a result partly of poor decision making, but partly also of past limitations of technology and understanding of needs. Indeed, many systems are designed to operate on their own. In one hospital visited there were 40 separate audit systems, not one of which had any links to other systems. The consequences include having to enter the same data more than once and a failure to reap the major benefits possible from sharing data.

Bias in the type of systems

47. There has been a bias towards administrative and financial systems, presumably because managers control budgets and have wanted reliable information with which to manage. The irony is that they have frequently failed to achieve their goal because the systems have not been fed by reliable data that are being used for operational clinical purposes.

Exhibit 10
Computer systems and the extent of linkage

Most systems are not linked to any other systems.

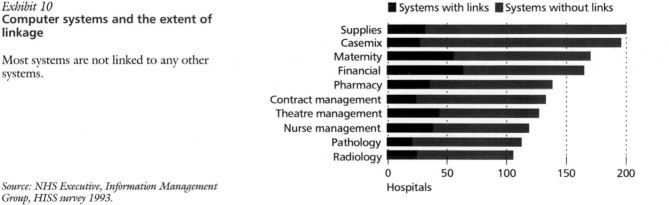

Source: NHS Executive, Information Management Group, HISS survey 1993.

Out-of-date systems

48. Many of the systems in widespread use are relatively old (Exhibit 11) and use outmoded software, despite often being dressed up to look more modern than they are. There are several causes for this: one is the present poor financial viability of the marketplace for vendors, with consequent under-investment in systems and attempts to extend the life of older systems due to lack of funds. Another is the structure of deals, where the initial cost must be held down to improve competitiveness; this encourages vendors to invest in their services rather than their core software. The consequences are:

◆ inflexibility, since systems written in older programming environments are generally more complicated to modify and more difficult to interface with other systems;

◆ increased running costs, since older environments require more and different skills to support, maintain, modify and interface;

◆ increased burden of learning for users, since older systems are generally less user-friendly and intuitive; and

◆ so-called 'technology lock-out', with older systems precluding the use of new technology, such as WIMP (Windows, Icons, Menus and Pointing devices).

Exhibit 11
The age of patient administration systems

Many of the systems in widespread use are relatively old.

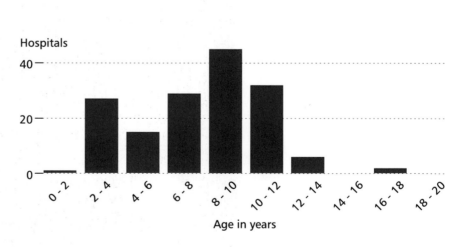

Source: Audit Commission analysis of 166 hospitals.

Badly designed systems

49. Lastly, systems may simply not function very well – they may, for example, be too small or inflexible, or may be difficult to access. One system found in the course of this study required clinicians to pass through six screens before reaching any clinically relevant data.

50. Systems may be poorly specified, particularly if there has been little staff involvement. A majority of nurses interviewed (70 per cent) were doubtful as to the overall benefits of the nurse care planning systems they used. The data captured were too detailed and the systems tried to satisfy conflicting needs. There is therefore less time available to spend with patients (Ref. 28).

51. Faced with these problems with the configuration and quality of systems, what can hospitals do? At first sight the answer appears to be 'not a lot' or 'learn from their mistakes next time'. This is wrong. There are some important principles that are worth establishing. And there are good and bad ways of learning from mistakes.

52. First and foremost, hospitals must have a plan for their information technology that is firmly rooted in their information strategy. Generally speaking, the plan should focus on clinical and operational systems. If systems are to assist the decisions in hospitals that really matter, they must:

- help with routine tasks (Case Study 3);

- group information by patient to assist the planning and delivery of care (Ref. 27);

- focus on and benefit patient care (Case Study 4);

- make ease of use a priority – in the short term this may mean adapting existing administrative systems through developing a clinically useful workstation;

- provide immediate benefits to users;

- provide routine outputs/reports for clinical audit and contract management;

- provide information to support cost-effective clinical practice and decisions;

- use common approaches to representation (classification and coding) of data; and

- link to PAS and other key departmental systems.

Case Study 3
Helping with routine tasks

Winchester and Eastleigh Healthcare
NHS Trust

In one hospital the information systems supported many of the key daily tasks of staff.

Doctor

Helps to:

- locate patients under care

- order investigations

- improve access to laboratory results (saves walking to ward or lab)

- increase the certainty that results are returned

- ease bed management and location

- produce timely discharge summaries

- update patient lists for ward rounds

Ward nurse

Helps to:

- save repeatedly checking patients' details

- improve structure of records

- support continuity of care for patients on transfer

Ward clerk

Helps to:

- support admissions to wards

- order meals and transport

- transfer notes when patients moved

- make records more legible

Occupational therapist

Helps to:

- aid transfers in and out

- help in planning work

- improve access to clinic information

- coordinate the care that patients receive

Case Study 4
Using clinical systems to benefit patient care

GeneCIS system, Morriston Hospital NHS Trust, Swansea

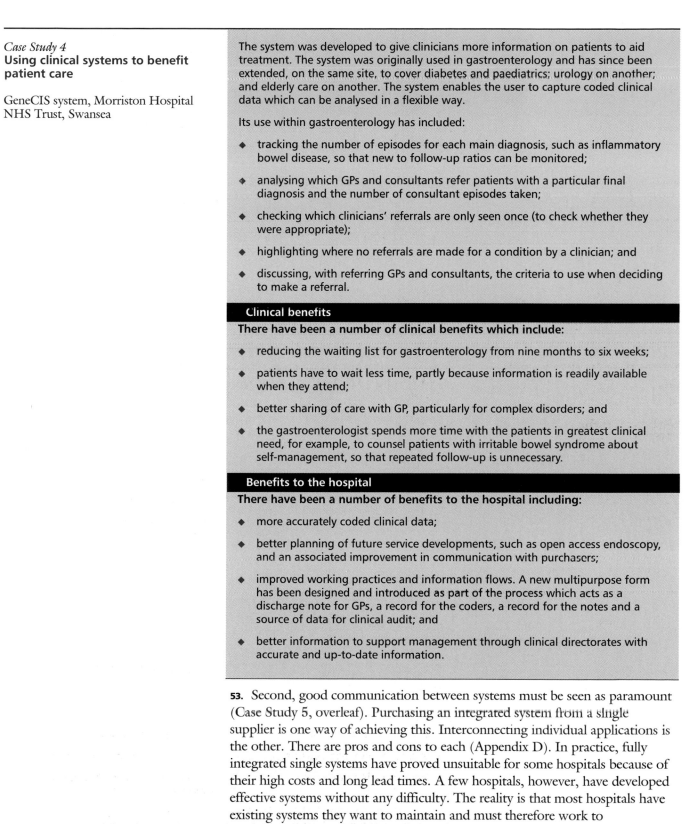

The system was developed to give clinicians more information on patients to aid treatment. The system was originally used in gastroenterology and has since been extended, on the same site, to cover diabetes and paediatrics; urology on another; and elderly care on another. The system enables the user to capture coded clinical data which can be analysed in a flexible way.

Its use within gastroenterology has included:

◆ tracking the number of episodes for each main diagnosis, such as inflammatory bowel disease, so that new to follow-up ratios can be monitored;

◆ analysing which GPs and consultants refer patients with a particular final diagnosis and the number of consultant episodes taken;

◆ checking which clinicians' referrals are only seen once (to check whether they were appropriate);

◆ highlighting where no referrals are made for a condition by a clinician; and

◆ discussing, with referring GPs and consultants, the criteria to use when deciding to make a referral.

Clinical benefits

There have been a number of clinical benefits which include:

◆ reducing the waiting list for gastroenterology from nine months to six weeks;

◆ patients have to wait less time, partly because information is readily available when they attend;

◆ better sharing of care with GP, particularly for complex disorders; and

◆ the gastroenterologist spends more time with the patients in greatest clinical need, for example, to counsel patients with irritable bowel syndrome about self-management, so that repeated follow-up is unnecessary.

Benefits to the hospital

There have been a number of benefits to the hospital including:

◆ more accurately coded clinical data;

◆ better planning of future service developments, such as open access endoscopy, and an associated improvement in communication with purchasers;

◆ improved working practices and information flows. A new multipurpose form has been designed and introduced as part of the process which acts as a discharge note for GPs, a record for the coders, a record for the notes and a source of data for clinical audit; and

◆ better information to support management through clinical directorates with accurate and up-to-date information.

53. Second, good communication between systems must be seen as paramount (Case Study 5, overleaf). Purchasing an integrated system from a single supplier is one way of achieving this. Interconnecting individual applications is the other. There are pros and cons to each (Appendix D). In practice, fully integrated single systems have proved unsuitable for some hospitals because of their high costs and long lead times. A few hospitals, however, have developed effective systems without any difficulty. The reality is that most hospitals have existing systems they want to maintain and must therefore work to interconnect them for reasons already stressed (Box 1, page 13). Corporate

Case Study 5
Good clinical communication requires good communication between systems

Burton Hospitals NHS Trust,
Burton-on-Trent

The hospital-wide system allows access to core clinical details of patients by staff caring for them. The easy access and transfer of patient details around the hospital helps continuity of care. This is particularly true for clinical staff based off the wards, such as physiotherapists and occupational therapists. The system is used by these staff to aid work planning: by looking up patient details when they receive a referral; helping to locate patients and their notes; and reporting details of treatment quickly to the wards. This saves time and ensures the patient receives consistent and coordinated care.

standards must therefore be adopted and adhered to, otherwise interconnection will rapidly become unaffordable, if not impossible. Lastly, a hospital that is suffering from old, inflexible or just downright poor quality systems has little option but to procure new ones – a process which carries its own risks.

System procurement and implementation

54. Most purchasers of systems have insufficient knowledge about possible vendors and of the distinguishing and unique features of the systems on offer. They will be involved in perhaps one procurement in their working lives. There are no safeguards to ensure that available software is fit for its purpose. Moreover, decisions on what system to acquire are often somewhat arbitrary, since no criteria for functionality have been agreed for evaluating alternatives. This often leaves cost as the main determinant. Vendors have a reputation for selling on the basis of 'demo-ware' that appears to work but in reality has yet to be developed; many procurements appear not to differentiate between developed and yet-to-be-developed features.

55. In fact, very few systems are purchased entirely 'as seen'; there is usually a requirement for some adaptation to local needs. But this raises a new difficulty since purchasers of systems are generally unable to specify precisely what they require at the outset of the procurement. There are aspects that are notoriously hard to define – for example, the look and feel of a system and its ease of use. Despite this, Department of Health procurement guidelines emphasise that a detailed specification is agreed and a fixed price contract entered into. That specification is then fixed until delivery. When the new system comes to be delivered, perhaps six to eight months after specification, the user needs and expectations have altered, often to the point where the solution supplied is deemed quite inappropriate. Whether or not the system meets the real needs has by then ceased to be an issue; it is the probity of the process that is being used to judge the success of the project.

56. Central guidance affects the procurement process adversely in other ways. Although some of the guidance is useful to hospitals, many of the numerous documents setting out best practice principles (Box 4) are long and cumbersome. This is partly necessary, because most people embarking on the procurement of a large system will be doing so for the first time. But, unfortunately, the documents and guidance may serve more to deter the would-be procurer of systems, than to help. In particular, the requirement for central approval of all projects costing over £1 million during their lifetime is

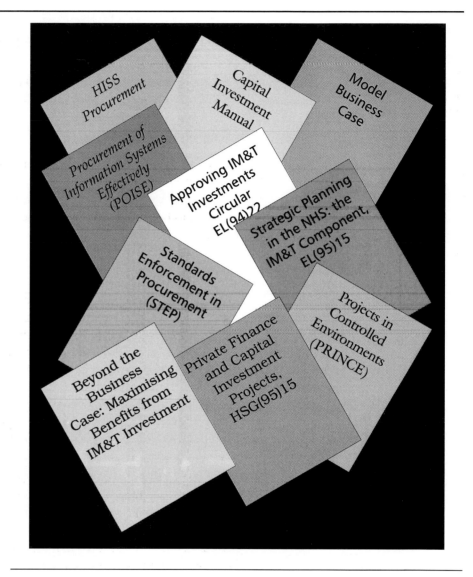

too bureaucratic (Ref. 29). The definition of cost includes capital, revenue financing and training and as such encompasses nearly every significant system in a hospital. Many hospitals spend disproportionate amounts of management time on gaining approvals for what are in reality comparatively small capital investments.

57. Systems purchasers also face problems with the quality of systems on offer – some of which are dubious. This is partly because the erratic nature of purchasing patterns, heavily influenced by changing central policy and fashion, has made it an unattractive market for serious investment and long-term development by system vendors. One consequence of this is the relatively old software packages being offered to purchasers. There are too many vendors for the size of the marketplace, and the cost to them of making each sale is too high for adequate investment to be sustained. Few vendors are bringing major new systems into the marketplace at the present time. Unless the marketplace is made more profitable to vendors, they will remain unable to invest adequately in order to enhance/upgrade/update their products.

58. Finally, once the system is procured, the problems of implementation begin. Conventional wisdom suggests that project managers should set goals, motivate and activate staff, and evaluate achievements; yet these are not prominent features of most implementation projects. Typically, information systems projects tend to be managed by an information technologist, often with no particular knowledge of healthcare or of organisational behaviour. Users are often involved too late to have any meaningful input into decisions and are thereby alienated. The problem of motivating staff for change is never easy, but is made more difficult when they are already alienated and where the person leading the change is not familiar with the fundamental issues that matter to them.

59. Improving this state of affairs will not be simple, but certain measures will help:

i   Users must be involved from the very beginnings of a project and included in the procurement process as well the implementation phase.

ii   The whole process must be 'owned' by senior management, who must also ensure that they are kept sufficiently informed of progress (see Chapter 3).

iii Users need to be given better access to up-to-date information about systems and supplies, particularly on how well they meet both technical and data standards. There needs to be better use made of external experts, such as those from the NHS Supplies Authority, who can draw on experience from many past procurements.

iv   Hospitals should develop formal mechanisms to ensure explicit consideration is given both to corporate information needs and to the hospital's overall information technology strategy in making a procurement decision (Exhibit 12).

Exhibit 12
Project control

Formal mechanisms are required to ensure that hospital needs for information drive the procurement process. This is an example used successfully in one hospital.

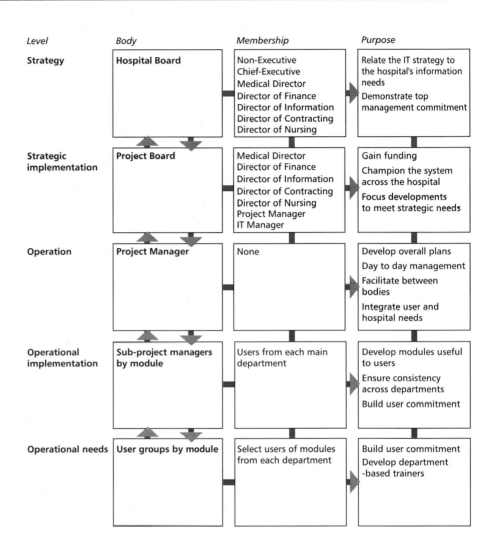

Level	Body	Membership	Purpose
Strategy	Hospital Board	Non-Executive Chief-Executive Medical Director Director of Finance Director of Information Director of Contracting Director of Nursing	Relate the IT strategy to the hospital's information needs Demonstrate top management commitment
Strategic implementation	Project Board	Medical Director Director of Finance Director of Information Director of Contracting Director of Nursing Project Manager IT Manager	Gain funding Champion the system across the hospital Focus developments to meet strategic needs
Operation	Project Manager	None	Develop overall plans Day to day management Facilitate between bodies Integrate user and hospital needs
Operational implementation	Sub-project managers by module	Users from each main department	Develop modules useful to users Ensure consistency across departments Build user commitment
Operational needs	User groups by module	Select users of modules from each department	Build user commitment Develop department -based trainers

Source: Audit Commission.

v   Much more flexibility needs to be introduced into the procurement and development process. A shift of emphasis in central guidelines is needed to encourage productive collaboration between purchaser and vendor – some form of partnership needs to be designed to solve the information management problem. The problems to be solved can be defined in the specification (rather than the solution itself forming the bulk of the specification), leaving the vendor able to adopt new technologies as they emerge. New ideas can be shared and discussed, and the planned deliverable modified. This serves both to enhance the deliverable as well as to keep expectations realistic. The procurement and development process becomes iterative, and the users can test the proposed solution and suggest modifications before the final deliverable is implemented (Case Study 6, overleaf).

vi   The costs of installing and implementing systems need to be fully estimated. Costs additional to the system itself can include:

- costs of educating and training staff;
- costs of training support staff;
- lost income resulting from the disruption;
- lost income from the non-availability of staff involved in training;
- reduced productivity whilst staff are learning the system; and
- costs of employing substitutes where required.

Much effort is frequently expended tying suppliers to original estimates, so running the risk of the system not meeting needs properly, when the really significant cost overruns are occurring in areas such as those just listed.

vii   Solutions to the problems of implementation depend, above all, on involving users from the beginning of the project (see **i** above) – in defining and specifying the requirements and in evaluating and choosing the successful system (Case Study 7).

viii   It is also important to ensure that the person who leads the implementation understands the core business the system is intended to serve and that they are respected by the staff who will have to use it. Involvement of clinical staff in this role is an excellent idea if it can be achieved. There is also much merit in hiring an advisor with experience, who knows the likely pitfalls.

60.   Many of the problems with systems and the way they interact with staff (data input and information use) are perpetuated by poor management. Managers frequently neither 'own' nor understand the problems and hope that hiring a good IT specialist and making money available will solve them. It will not. Senior managers (and indeed boards) have a duty to be fully involved in the planning and staffing aspects of information management and IT – responsibilities that are the subject of the next chapter.

Case Study 6
Partnership with suppliers

Glan Clwyd District General Hospital
NHS Trust, Clwyd

A full HIS system including patient administration, ward ordering and results reporting, and casemix was introduced, from procurement to implementation, in 18 months. This was done by establishing a partnership with the suppliers which depended on:

- an early clarification of roles, the hospital and users determining 'what' and the suppliers determining 'how'. The supplier's IT project manager became the technical manager – the hospital signed up early to a broad vision based on demonstrations, with the detail agreed later

- high quality staff were committed to the project from the hospital and the supplier for the full duration of the project which enabled settled relationships to develop

- an early agreement on the key milestones and close monitoring to check on their achievement

- agreeing a mechanism to discuss openly and solve problems through working together

Case Study 7
Gaining staff commitment through involvement

Burton Hospitals NHS Trust,
Burton-on-Trent

The hospital is a general hospital with 450 beds and employs 1900 staff. A hospital-wide system was introduced over a period of two years. The project manager acted as a facilitator between the different staff using the system. He coordinated user needs, made sure they could be integrated with the hospital's broader objectives and translated them into specifications for operational systems. In this process user needs were kept separate from the technology issues and by clarifying them and making them explicit this meant they were key drivers in the development of the system. Staff were involved throughout in:

◆ reviewing the capability of existing systems;

◆ discussing their information needs with the project team;

◆ deciding whether and how to develop the existing systems;

◆ writing the Statement of Need for the part(s) of the system they would use;

◆ helping choose the new systems, informed by site visits and system demonstrations;

◆ ensuring priority was given to providing immediate user benefits, such as having rapid access to test results, information for clinics and an easy means to produce patient and GP letters (especially for outpatient clinics);

◆ emphasising ease of use in the choice and tailoring of the system;

◆ meeting chosen supplier to outline detailed needs;

◆ part-funding the project through the voluntary use of their clinical department's equipment budgets;

◆ choosing project managers from their departments to lead the development of specific modules;

◆ forming user groups to help design modules and the data to capture; and

◆ acting as trainers to lead the development of use in each department.

Recommendations

Hospital boards should:

1 ensure there is an overall hospital information strategy which is regularly reviewed, relates to the hospital's business and is endorsed by healthcare purchasers.

They should take steps to improve data quality through:

2 facilitating data collection by adopting hospital-wide standards for data definition and codes;

3 involving clinical staff in data collection;

4 making medical consultants responsible for the quality of clinical data and coding;

5 initiating a system of quality assurance for all data; and

6 using appropriate technologies to simplify data capture.

They should enhance the use made of currently available information by:

7 educating staff about the extended uses of operational data (in addition to direct patient care) and their importance to the viability of their department and the hospital as a whole;

8 enabling staff to define their own information needs and the purposes for which that information is required;

9 investing in skills and technology for transforming available data into usable information; and

10 ensuring that adequate terminals and processing power are provided to cope with the demands at peak times.

They should ensure future success in procurement and implementation of systems by:

11 ensuring that there is a hospital technology strategy, which is regularly reviewed to keep abreast of changes in technology, a part of which addresses the issues of the standards that will be used;

12 ensuring that clinical and non-clinical systems are developed side by side and not independent of each other; recognising that operational data from clinical systems is essential to feed administrative and financial systems;

13 ensuring that the present and probable future needs for linkages and integration between systems are identified;

14 seeking assistance from auditors and industry advisors to implement the requirements of the procurement process in a more flexible way, focusing especially on the nature of the relationship with the chosen supplier; and

15 ensuring that the full costs of procurement and implementation are recognised and adequate provision is made for them.

The Department of Health and the Welsh Office should:

16 specify all the benefits, not solely financial, which may form part of the business case for development of hospital information systems;

17 ensure that experiences in implementing systems are evaluated, benefits identified (especially any improvements in patient care) and lessons are shared across the NHS;

18 support the linking between intra-hospital systems by defining standard data sets that meet the hospitals' immediate needs;

19 take steps (possibly including direct financial support) to ensure the widespread adoption of appropriate standards in the shortest possible time;

20 provide access to comprehensive and up-to-date information on available systems, the standards they incorporate and the functions they fulfil, as well as reference sites where they are installed;

21 review how current guidance on procurement is being used and modify it to meet the hospitals' needs;

22 examine how certification and quality assurance of software can be implemented; and

23 review the documentation on procurement provided to hospitals and ensure that, as well as detailed reference materials, simple and easy-to-use handbooks are provided for those who only need to understand the concepts, purposes and principles.

3 The Responsibilities of Management

Many of the problems are perpetuated by poor management. Managers need to grasp the key issues. Improved planning is also required.

Specialist IT staff are required to manage developments. Other staff need education and training to get benefit from using systems.

The security and confidentiality of patient data must be carefully protected.

'Many trusts are held back by a vicious circle of poor understanding of information issues, negative attitudes and inadequate representation at the top of the organisation'

Management knowledge, understanding, leadership and commitment

61. In order to progress in the key areas described in the previous chapter (data collection, information use, systems procurement and implementation), the board and senior management of a hospital will need to attend to some essential prerequisites:

◆ they must ensure that they fully understand the value of information, and show leadership and commitment in developing it;

◆ there must be a robust mechanism for planning systems investment and development so they are fully driven by the information needs of the hospital's clinical and business priorities, and so that key aspects are coordinated trust-wide;

◆ they must see that the hospital has the right specialist staff, and take steps so that all staff have the necessary information and IT skills, and positive attitudes towards IT; and

◆ they also have a special duty with respect to security and confidentiality, because of the highly sensitive nature of health data.

62. Chief executives, boards and senior managers often fail to appreciate the potential benefits of good information or the costs and negative impact of poor information. They perceive the principal aim of IT investments as simply being to reduce costs. There is little understanding of the potential of better information management to improve the 'core business' of patient care and in some situations, no doubt, ensure the viability of the hospital. This lack of understanding derives in part from many managers' experiences of introducing computers to hospitals, experiences which have led in some instances to unhelpful attitudes towards investment in information management and systems.

◆ Central funding has left some managers with a 'free good' mentality towards systems development, which can become a substitute for thought and careful planning.

◆ Investments are too often justified purely in terms of immediate savings, frequently based on short-term staff reductions, but which in practice are rarely realistic or achievable.

◆ Compliance with formal procurement processes (some of which are necessary for probity and accountability) can become a goal in its own right, to the detriment of other goals, such as having systems that add value.

◆ The focus of investments is on buying hardware and technology rather than on the need for staff to gain skills in information management and the use of systems, or on meeting the needs of patient care.

◆ The general lack of knowledge and skills, and the absence of a formal network of IT professionals, means that many hospitals repeat each others' mistakes (rather than learning from them) and have a naive approach to procurement.

63. These attitudes are often shared by many of those purchasing healthcare services, who may have to approve investments in information systems by provider units (Ref. 30).

'Many trusts are held back by a vicious circle of poor understanding of information issues, negative attitudes and inadequate representation at the top of the organisation'

64. One of the consequences of these negative attitudes and lack of understanding of information management is that many hospitals do not have the issues properly represented at board level. Only 21 per cent of NHS hospitals have specific directors of information, of whom about half have a place on the board (Ref. 31). In most other hospitals information services are responsible to the Finance director, who answers for information matters at the board.

65. Yet the representation of information issues at board level is crucial for reaching balanced, high quality decisions on development of information management and systems. Some of the consequences of not having information issues directly represented to the board are:

♦ poor decisions on the distribution of resources to information management balanced against alternative calls on the available funds;

♦ crucial decisions about information management strategies being left to individual departments. These compromise attempts to achieve integrity of information within the hospital and attempts to ensure that systems support the overall needs of the hospital;

♦ an over-emphasis on financial and strategic information systems at the expense of clinical and operational systems; and

♦ perpetuation of the negative attitudes and poor understanding that underlie the lack of board representation.

Improving leadership

66. Many trusts are held back by a vicious circle of poor understanding of information issues, negative attitudes and inadequate representation, right at the top of the organisation. To break this circle, boards and senior managers must:

♦ acquire a broad understanding of health information and grasp a few key points;

♦ openly acknowledge the importance of information and give a clear lead to other staff through active involvement; and

♦ ensure that information management has proper executive representation on the board, and that the board in turn owns responsibility for it.

67. Boards and senior managers must first of all educate themselves about health information and the necessary underlying technology. They can for example:

♦ arrange seminars/awaydays with either their own specialist staff or failing that, outside speakers;

♦ make visits to other hospitals/sites where information is being well managed; and

♦ ensure that relevant experience is present among the board's non-executives.

68. In the course of developing their understanding, it is important that boards and senior managers grasp certain key points, all of which are stressed in this report. Most notably, they should understand:

◆ that the prime purpose of clinical information is to support patient care;

◆ that good clinical information will also improve management and contracting decisions;

◆ the need for the trust to be able to share information with other bodies, particularly those providing community and primary care services;

◆ the absolute necessity of adopting standards in some areas of data definition and technology;

◆ the importance of planning and prioritising information needs; and

◆ the need for confidentiality and security of patients' personal information.

69. Understanding the issues is necessary. Being seen to act on them is even more important. Boards need to demonstrate their commitment to information as a valuable resource. When they do this, implementation is more likely to be successful (Case Study 8).

70. Lastly, boards must ensure that there is proper leadership of the information function itself. But the chief information officer (or equivalent) will not be fully effective unless he or she has good access to the board. Equally crucial, this individual must understand clinical information as well as information systems and technology. Only then will he or she be able to establish the necessary dialogue between those who run the 'core business' of clinical care and those responsible for management decisions such as investment priorities.

Planning

71. Trusts require a strategic view of their information needs: which matter most; and which will give the best return in terms of efficiency and effectiveness of services. In the absence of such a plan, systems development will be uncoordinated and fail to yield the most benefit.

Case Study 8
Leadership from the top

Burton Hospitals NHS Trust,
Burton-on-Trent

The hospital had embarked on the successful implementation of a hospital-wide system. A main reason for this had been the strong leadership provided by the hospital's board. The chief executive and medical director, in particular, had taken a close interest. They had:

◆ visited sites and suppliers to identify the potential in using technology;

◆ shown commitment to a vision based around improving direct patient care;

◆ recognised that many of the benefits were likely to relate to quality of care rather than immediate cost-savings;

◆ developed a number of 'clinical champions' to promote interest in the development of information systems; and

◆ actively involved board members in the implementation through attending the steering group and monitoring the impact of the system.

72. Most hospitals visited by the Audit Commission in the course of this study had purchased their major systems before they developed an information strategy. Few had identified clear objectives or measures of success at the start of projects. Even when they had such measures, it was exceptional for them to refer to the quality of patient care.

Improving planning

73. A trust's strategy for information systems and technology must be driven by its information needs. It is good practice to review care processes and adjust the need for information accordingly, before the introduction of new systems (Exhibit 13) (Ref. 32). In one hospital visited, although patient information was already recorded on the patient administration system, it was also manually recorded in seven different places including the ward register, discharge register, theatre register, disease register and day diary.

74. The strategic information plan must make it clear which decisions can be left to local or departmental discretion and which require compliance with corporate rules. The integration of information within and beyond the hospital requires common use of technical and data standards. This is an area where corporate policy is essential to ensure that systems converge to permit complete integration of information over a period of time. It is not an area

Exhibit 13
Reviewing care processes and information flows

There must be a commitment to reviewing care processes and adjusting the need for information accordingly, as part of the introduction of new systems.

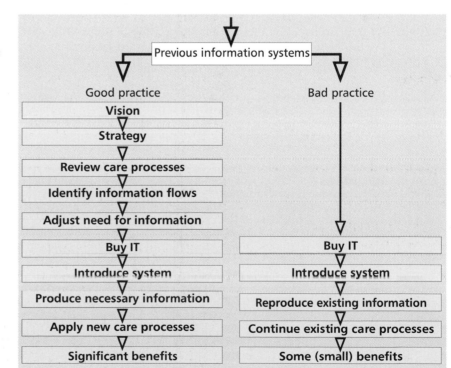

Source: Audit Commission.

where departments and directorates can be allowed to follow their own directions. Nor is it something which can be delegated to information departments; there must be wide involvement and consultation throughout the organisation and the outcome must be understood, debated and approved at board level and in other management committees.

75. The options for financing investments in information systems need to be reviewed. Government regulations now require trusts to consider leasing and joint partnerships with the private sector before NHS capital is committed (Refs. 33 - 35). Also investments must be backed by a business case which:

◆ considers a wide range of options;

◆ brings all relevant costs and income into an assessment of net present value; and

◆ shows that the decision is in line with the needs of users and commissioning bodies.

76. One of the best ways of improving any planning process is to ensure that previous mistakes are learned from. Despite this, there has been little evaluation of information management, systems or services. The information about implementation of systems that is fed back to management often has not been objective and, as a consequence, top managers generally have a poor grasp of information management and the value and impact of systems at the workplace. Few of the main sites visited formally monitored the impact of systems. Nationally only eight per cent of nursing information systems have had formal evaluations with a written report (Ref. 36). And most current evaluation is focused on financial and manpower benefits, rather than benefits to patient care or professional satisfaction and productivity (Ref. 37).

77. Plans for implementing new systems or services should include proposals for monitoring and evaluation. The benefits expected should be pre-defined and the measures to be used should be clear and explicit. The result of such evaluation should be considered by all those involved in the decisions and plans, including, in some cases, the trust board.

Staffing implications

78. Trusts have two main challenges in relation to staffing aspects of information management and technology. First, they must ensure that they have enough specialist staff with the necessary understanding and skills. Second, they must ensure that all staff, or at least a large majority, are equipped to use information and information systems productively.

Specialist staff

79. Specialist information staff are involved in education, training and user support, as well as installing, maintaining, modifying and operating computer systems. They often work in an 'information systems and technology' department.

80. It is vital to ensure that such a department has equally strong links and accountability to clinical as to financial and administrative departments. The

'Even the best system will be a failure if staff are not committed'

key qualification for the director of such a department is knowledge, understanding and experience in health information management; a working knowledge of healthcare and of information technology is also important. The essential view of this department should be of the users as clients, from whom its business comes and on whom its continued existence must depend; approachability, helpfulness and ability to speak to clients in non-technical terms are essential attributes. Evaluation of the service given by departments and their 'helpdesks' should be undertaken regularly through user surveys.

81. In practice few of the staff of these specialist departments have any direct experience of clinical care. Indeed, the information systems and technology department is very frequently found to be tied to finance and administration rather than clinical services: this was true of 43 per cent of the main study sites. Such a situation usually occurs because computers were originally applied to financial management of the hospital. This often makes it difficult for them to establish rapport with clinical staff (Ref. 31) and to provide them with operational advice and support. Needs for financial information tend to be given priority over clinical needs, if only because the technical staff can better understand the issues and the solutions and can therefore be positively supportive of proposals.

82. There is no shortage of pure information technologists. The problem trusts face is finding staff with a working understanding of healthcare and of clinical and business information needs. The short supply of such 'healthcare informatics' staff is compounded by the relatively low pay rates that most trusts feel obliged to offer and by the lack of a recognised career path for them.

83. Trusts have two ways of solving this problem. They can pay the market rate for the right staff (which means either paying above the normal NHS rates or employing consultants or advisors on short-term contracts). Alternatively, they can try to develop and educate existing staff – either information technologists or clinical staff – to give them the necessary additional skills and knowledge.

All users

84. Most staff now use systems and the information from them. It is essential that they have the skills to make the systems do what they, the users, want. Yet around half of staff interviewed felt they received insufficient training: 35 per cent of medical staff, 44 per cent of nurses and 60 per cent of business managers. As a result, staff feel inadequate and are reluctant to explore and make full use of any system. This makes the realisation of benefits more difficult.

85. Lack of skills and knowledge are frequently compounded by negative attitudes towards information systems. Experience in other sectors has clearly shown that the key factor in whether an information system is successful or not is the attitude of the staff towards it. Even the best system will be a failure if staff are not committed. The extent to which the facilities within an information system are used varies, but systems are frequently found where

less than ten per cent of their capabilities are being used. Healthcare staff, and especially those in senior positions, often have a choice as to whether or not they use a system (Ref. 38). Where staff are negative and unwilling to experiment, systems become under-used – a recent survey of US hospitals found that many systems were used to less than a quarter of their capability (Ref. 39). There is also likely to be growth in user resistance which is a common cause of computer system failures (Ref. 40).

86. Often, there is an intrinsic lack of interest in information management and systems amongst clinical staff. Many clinicians see their role as limited to the clinical care of patients and reject the notion that they have a wider role in managing information and managing the business of the hospital. One nurse interviewed said: 'I became a nurse to care for patients, not to play around with computers'. Part of the reason for such attitudes has been a lack of leadership from professional bodies, resulting in a poor attendance at education and training sessions, as well as at conferences on information management. A recent national event for medical staff attracted fewer than 40 clinicians. At the main annual conference for healthcare computing, fewer than ten per cent of delegates were clinical staff. This compares to a similar conference in the USA, where approximately half of the 3,000 delegates are clinical staff. This situation is made worse by a lack of clear leadership; there are numerous groups (at least five in the UK) who compete for professionals interested in clinical computing.

87. Trusts can take various actions to improve this situation. They need to ensure that all staff receive necessary education and training and that there is adequate user support for systems, and they need to monitor and encourage positive attitudes towards information.

Education and training

88. Budgets for information and systems generally make insufficient allowance for training. Hospitals should plan to invest a significant amount (some have advocated 30 per cent) of the costs of any development in education and training of staff. Training should be:

- job-related – in order to motivate staff the use of systems must be seen to result in immediate benefits to their work;

- flexible – where necessary, individual tutoring may be required; individuals will learn at different rates and some may wish to learn the system in their own time;

- progressive – to allow staff to develop their use of a system;

- ongoing – to permit new staff to acquire the necessary knowledge, understanding and skills;

- pro-active – searching out those with problems to offer guidance;

- non-threatening – showing sensitivity about mixing different staff, in case some feel vulnerable when being trained alongside colleagues;

◆ effective – carried out in an appropriate place, preferably away from the work environment to avoid distractions and interruptions; and

◆ evaluated – to determine the effectiveness and acceptability and to change the emphasis and approach as necessary.

User support

89. There must be adequate support for staff using any system if the full benefits are to be realised and negative attitudes avoided. There is wide variation in the numbers of specialist information and IT staff employed by hospitals (Exhibit 14). This is only partly a reflection of hospital sizes and the ratio of specialist staff to users ranged from 1 to 80 up to 1 to 300 in the sites visited in this study. In any case, staff often prefer to turn to those who work with them as their first point of contact for help, rather than to a computer helpdesk.

90. Support is customarily separated into first level (general knowledge, such as how to switch on, access routine functions, etc.) and second level (involving detailed knowledge of the software and/or technical issues). It is not cost-effective to use skilled technologists in first-level support operations; this should be delegated to staff who are experienced and have been provided with additional education and training to be able to deal with most routine problems. These 'computer first aid' staff should be distributed throughout the

Exhibit 14
Investment in support staff

There is wide variation in the numbers of specialist information and IT staff.

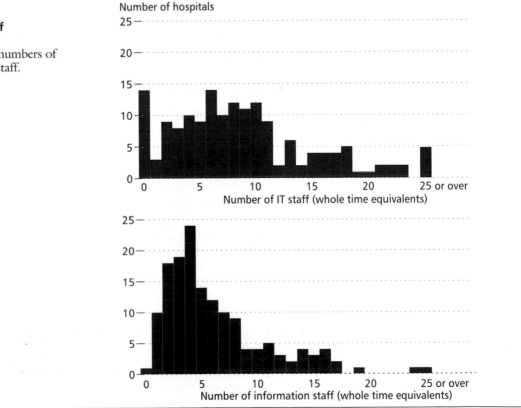

Source: Audit Commission analysis.

Case Study 9
Providing ongoing training and support

Burton Hospitals NHS Trust,
Burton-on-Trent

> When the hospital was introducing a hospital-wide system it made a commitment to extensive investment in training, backed by resources. This entailed not only initial training but also follow-up training and pro-active support for users from a variety of sources.
>
> Core trainers within each ward and department were nominated for each of the system modules. These were trained on each of the modules and then returned to their workplace to train their colleagues.
>
> ◆ They provided support on the wards and in departments, helping, advising and reassuring their colleagues.
>
> ◆ Time was taken to understand and sort out individual problems.
>
> ◆ Staff were taken away from their work environment to train.
>
> ◆ Training manuals and guidance for specific tasks were developed.

hospital, in easy reach of all users, with job descriptions that recognise this activity and with rates of pay that recognise the added skills involved (Case Study 9).

91. Effective second-level support involves having a helpdesk to provide a single point of contact for all users. The helpdesk must see the users as its clients and measure its success on the basis of the number of users whose problems it resolves fully in the minimum time. Evaluation of the helpfulness of helpdesks is vital.

Managing attitudes

92. The most important thing trusts can do is ensure that systems work and the information they yield is useful and reliable. If staff are sceptical or negative for good reason, there may be little that can (or indeed should) be done to talk them out of it. But, if negative attitudes are unfounded, it is worth trying to correct the situation. Senior managers must set an example by using, and being seen to use, systems themselves and being positive about information. And the potential benefits of using systems and information must be clearly communicated to staff. If this is done and if staff are adequately trained and supported, and involved in developments early on, then negative attitudes should cease to be the major impediment to progress that they have become in some trusts.

Security and confidentiality of health information

93. The fourth area to which boards and senior management must attend and for which they must accept full responsibility is ensuring the security and confidentiality of data. Although not in a strict sense essential to gaining benefits from information management, the associated technology does, as has already been pointed out (para 9) increase the risk to personal data and this is causing growing concern. Formal and legal standards are being developed in response, supported by recent guidance (Refs. 41 and 42).

94. Yet, despite the general recognition of the sensitivity of health information, the record of practice in hospitals in England and Wales has been variable. There are, for example, numerous recorded instances of medical records being left in corridors unattended, in record stores which are unsecured, sent to rubbish dumps without being shredded, disclosed to third parties without authorisation and so on (examples of the types of lapses of trust are referred to in the Audit Commission's 1995 report *Setting the Records Straight*) (Ref. 26).

95. The sometimes cavalier approach towards paper records seems in danger of spilling over to computerised information. Problems encountered at study sites included:

◆ confusion about which members of staff are authorised to access what information;

◆ inadequate staff education about the needs for and implications of personal privacy;

◆ poor privacy when personal data are being collected;

◆ inadequate control of access to systems (multi-user passwords, unchanged passwords, unused terminals left logged on, no physical security of data stores or system terminals etc.);

◆ information collected for one purpose (e.g. clinical care) being used for another without authorisation (e.g. patient registration details used for fundraising campaigns (Ref. 26); information disclosed to third parties); and

◆ failure to take action against employees for breach of privacy and a lack of any legislative base for bringing such an action (unless bribery or corruption are involved).

96. In response to these problems, and in order to promote confidence amongst patients and practitioners, boards and senior managers should first ensure that for the long term all new systems acquisitions include a full range of access controls, audit trails etc. designed to prevent and detect unauthorised access to data.

97. Second, they should take active steps to develop policies and rules that protect personal data while keeping it readily available for legitimate use. Such steps may include:

◆ assembling a list of personal information stored on all computer systems or networks;

◆ ensuring that all systems, large and small, networked or stand-alone, are subject to an overall security policy, including rules for access to data systems and contracts (including penalties) governing their use;

◆ developing hospital-wide policies on data collection, in particular, reviewing data collection forms for consistency with privacy principles;

◆ developing policies on disclosure of information, review of any reports or summaries provided to third parties;

◆ use of appropriate physical protective measures and data back-up/copying procedures to protect stored data from loss or damage;

◆ ensuring that stored data is readily available to authorised users at all times; providing for systems and data to be duplicated where necessary to ensure continued availability; and

◆ promotion of staff awareness of the need for security.

Recommendations

Hospital boards should:

1 ensure that board members and senior staff understand the critical importance of information management;

2 play an active role in the planning, procurement and development of major hospital-wide systems;

3 consider the full range of options to finance systems;

4 ensure that benefits to patients and clinical staff are fully recognised when investment decisions are being made;

5 ensure closer links between information management staff and clinical departments;

6 address the reporting chain of information management so it is adequately represented at board level. The director of information needs good access to the board;

7 review information flows and care processes to take advantage of any improvements that computerisation can bring;

8 ensure early, direct involvement of users and good project management;

9 ensure that the implementation and impact of systems are fully evaluated;

10 allocate adequate funds for staff education and training, including attendance at conferences and seminars;

11 review and evaluate the performance of information management staff; and

12 develop a security and privacy policy for the hospital and take steps to ensure that staff are familiar and compliant with its provisions.

Professional bodies should:

13 build up internal expertise on information management and systems technology;

14 coordinate their efforts; and

15 take a leadership role for their members in promoting knowledge, understanding and development of information systems and technology.

Commissioning authorities should:

16 actively support the development of and investment in information systems that promote improvements in the efficiency and quality of care provided by acute hospitals.

The Department of Health and the Welsh Office should:

17 support trusts in educating and training their staff in information management, systems and technology; and

18 review security guidance.

4 The Way Forward

As a first step, management need to assess the key issues in their hospital.

Local audits are taking place to explore the application of the principles in this report to local hospitals.

98. This report has identified some of the problems with information management and systems and some potential solutions. It has concentrated particularly on the importance of the board and senior management playing an active and central role in all information developments. Embracing the issues raised in Chapter 3 is an essential step in this direction, but alone it is not enough. Management have to know where they are starting from by comparison with other trusts and which are the key areas and issues that they must address first.

99. It would be ideal if there were a simple standard solution to these problems, but there is not. Every institution is different, with different organisation, needs and legacy of investment. An information management system that can solve the problems at one stroke does not exist. But there is a method, which involves working through the issues and learning from the process and its findings.

100. Managers and board members who have read this report will want to know whether their hospital is doing well and where it could do better. To help in this a number of key issues have been identified below. They are not the only important issues, nor are there any 'right' answers. The intention is to provide some qualitative indication of strengths and weaknesses and to raise awareness of issues that may not have been adequately addressed.

101. Auditors appointed by the Audit Commission are currently looking at whether trusts are obtaining value for money from their investment in information management and technology. These local audits, which are outlined at the end of this chapter, explore locally many of the issues covered in this report.

Reviewing information issues

Reviewing information issues in your hospital

1 Management checklist

- Is the board adequately aware of the importance of efficient and effective information management and sufficiently informed to be able to make decisions about investments? If not, does it have access to a source of reliable advice and guidance?

- Is there a strategic plan for information? If so, has the board read it, understood it and 'signed up to' it?

- Are board IM&T priorities driven by patient care needs as much as administration needs?

- Is there a hospital-wide body that determines priorities for information? Does it get a sympathetic hearing at the board? Are information issues well represented at board level, by someone with a clear remit?

- Are there strong links between information services and clinical services (e.g. information staff dedicated to a clinical directorate or a clinician as an information director)? Are these links at least as strong as those of information services with the finance department?

- Does the board recognise that investment in information management systems may be justified by benefits to patient care, service quality, unit productivity and staff job satisfaction, as well as by direct money or manpower savings? Has it actively encouraged any projects of this type?

- In the last year have board members visited any other hospitals or events such as conferences to help improve their understanding of information management issues?

2 Staffing checklist

- Does the board understand that investing in education and training is as important as investing in hardware and software?

- Of the total expenditure on any information project is a significant amount assigned to education, training and development?

- Is training seen as an ongoing exercise rather than a 'one-off'?

- Do those with education and training responsibilities have adequate knowledge of the daily work of the staff they are training? Is the impact of their courses objectively and regularly evaluated?

- What steps are taken to ensure that all staff, especially clinical staff, attend vital education and training sessions? Are self-study materials and resources available?

- Are staff educated in how the information they collect is important for the management of the hospital and is used by others in the hospital and outside?

3 Data collection and information checklist

◆ Is data collection planned (i.e. data collected only where there is a specific defined use for them)? Are most items of data collected useful to those collecting them? For instance, are many data items derived as a by-product of the process of caring for a patient?

◆ Is the extra burden on staff of data capture for administrative purposes fully appreciated by managers? How much time roughly does each category of staff spend recording and entering data?

◆ Is there any inventory of all the data held by the hospital, who holds it, and where?

◆ Is there a process for assuring the quality of all the data collected?

◆ Is the proportion of incorrectly coded diagnoses and procedures measured?

◆ Are managers aware of broad measures of success in the use of information. Do they, for example, know:

– how quickly GPs find out from the hospital about inpatient and outpatient services received by their patients?

– how long the typical wait is for discharge letters to GPs?

– whether GPs and community care service providers are entirely happy with the information they receive, in terms of timeliness, legibility, quality or adequacy?

◆ Is the information provided to the board well presented and easily understood? Is it relevant to the board's deliberations and decisions?

◆ Are specific data readily available to support or refute complaints from purchasers, providers and/or patients?

◆ Are developing areas such as clinical management and marketing well supported? For instance, is it easy to analyse demand for the hospital's services by GP practice?

4 Security and confidentiality checklist

◆ Are there clear policies and procedures in place to ensure patient data are kept secure and confidential? Are the staff fully aware of these policies (e.g. through mandatory courses of instruction, possibly with a test of comprehension)? Are penalties for non-compliance specified?

◆ Are there mechanisms in place to check for compliance with the above policies and to monitor abuses of confidentiality? Are audits carried out frequently?

◆ Is there an effective policy on patient access to their own data? Does it work? How long, on average, do patients have to wait for a decision? Have there been complaints about ease of access?

◆ Is the medical records store physically secured? Are the identities of those requesting records checked before access is granted? Is a log kept of all accesses to records?

◆ How often does a consultation take place without the record?

◆ Do all computer systems (mainframe and microcomputers, networked and stand-alone) have the normal range of security counter-measures in place (e.g. access control, frequent password changes, no shared or 'ward' logins, time-outs on terminals, frequent back-ups, disaster recovery plans, audit trails, roll-back facilities etc.)?

◆ Are there policies for periods of retention and procedures for destruction of records in place? Are they observed?

5 Systems checklist

◆ Are the main information systems seen as saving time and being easy to use by ward nurses and medical staff?

◆ Can users always easily find a terminal when required?

◆ Are basic patient details (such as name and address) easily transferred between patient administration, nursing and audit systems?

◆ Are there microcomputers and networks in directorates/departments? If so, are they linked to central systems?

◆ Is there an appropriate balance between expenditure on administrative and financial systems and on those systems designed to support patient care and services?

◆ Have hospital-wide standards been adopted for technical issues and for data representation, classification and coding? If so, do all systems comply with them?

◆ Is technical documentation of systems, developments and modifications maintained up to date at all times?

◆ Are all applications used in connection with patient care (including those on microcomputers) checked for suitability of purpose and integrity of performance? Is there a log kept of modifications to operational systems?

6 Procurement and implementation checklist

◆ Does a board member chair the implementation group of major projects?

◆ Does the board receive regular information enabling it to monitor the progress of any system procurement and implementation (e.g. for cost over-run, timetable slippage)?

◆ Is there adequate knowledge and understanding within the organisation of POISE, STEP and PRINCE or equivalent guides to procurement and implementation issues? If not, is there a source of help available?

◆ Where there is a project in progress, has the leader a wider background than technology? Has he/she any working experience of healthcare provision?

◆ Are those who are to be affected by any new system involved early and actively in its specification and selection?

◆ Could the relationship with selected system(s) suppliers be described as a partnership?

◆ Is there a formal evaluation of the impact of information systems? Is the information fed back to influence future initiatives?

7 Information management and technology departments checklist

◆ Are the IM&T staff more aligned with the computing needs of administrative or clinical staff? Amongst them are there any with backgrounds in healthcare delivery?

◆ Is there a 'helpdesk'? Is it evaluated regularly by users? How capable, helpful and friendly is the IM&T department as a whole perceived as being towards other key staff?

◆ Does the IM&T department have responsibility for all computing systems in the institution or is its domain limited to the centralised systems only?

The Audit

Local audits will focus on many of the issues raised by these questions. They will assess the provision of information and information systems in acute hospitals, including those that support the hospitals' links to purchasers and GPs. There is a three-phased approach (Exhibit 15).

National data collection

All NHS hospitals provided data in response to a request from local auditors. The focus of the questionnaire was on information service and technology costs, staffing patterns and types of systems in use. These data were assembled and analysed centrally by the Commission and the results have been returned to local auditors for use in the audit overview (see below).

The audit overview

The overview is based upon a number of questionnaires, reviews of key trust documentation and a series of structured interviews. This will enable the trust to compare itself with hospitals of a similar type and size. The overview will examine five key areas:

- costs – identify each hospital's information and information technology (IT) costs and compare them to other hospitals (Exhibit 16);
- information for operational staff – assess the provision of key operational information for doctors, nurses and management and identify priority areas for improvement;
- patient administration – assess the effectiveness of the key elements of the patient administration process and suggest changes to reduce duplication of information gathered;
- reliability of information – measure purchasers' views of the quality of information for use in contracting and suggest improvements; and
- strategy – assess the effectiveness of the hospital's information and IT strategies and how they support its business needs.

The auditor will produce a report detailing the findings from the overview and indicating priority areas for action either from the follow-up audit or by the hospital.

Follow-up review

With the agreement of the hospital, further work will be undertaken to follow through the priorities identified by the overview. These will cover key areas such as:

- the information requirements of hospital management and clinical directorates;
- the effectiveness of the patient administrative process;
- ward information needs;
- contracting and billing; and
- effectiveness of the IT acquisition process.

Exhibit 15
Audit structure

There is a three phased approach to local audits.

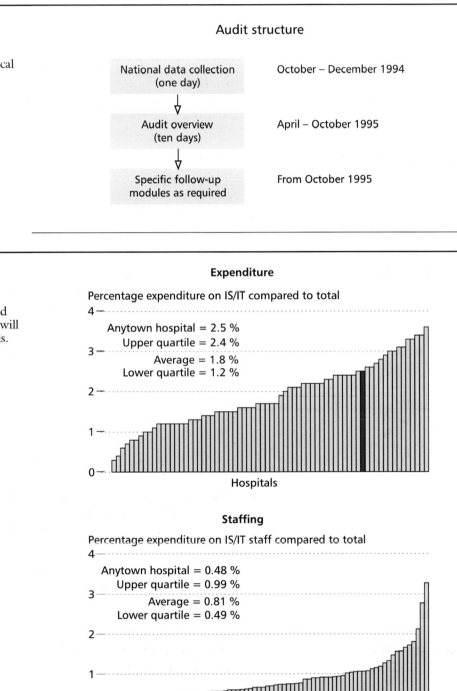

Audit structure

National data collection (one day)	October – December 1994
Audit overview (ten days)	April – October 1995
Specific follow-up modules as required	From October 1995

Source: Audit Commission.

Exhibit 16
Benchmarking

Your hospital's information system and information technology (IS/IT) costs will be compared to other, similar hospitals.

Expenditure

Percentage expenditure on IS/IT compared to total

Anytown hospital = 2.5 %
Upper quartile = 2.4 %
Average = 1.8 %
Lower quartile = 1.2 %

Hospitals

Staffing

Percentage expenditure on IS/IT staff compared to total

Anytown hospital = 0.48 %
Upper quartile = 0.99 %
Average = 0.81 %
Lower quartile = 0.49 %

Hospitals

Source: Audit Commission analysis of acute trusts (non-teaching).

Appendix A

Site visit

Main visits were made to the following acute units by the study team:
- Addenbrooke's NHS Trust, Cambridge
- United Bristol Healthcare NHS Trust, Bristol
- Burton Hospitals NHS Trust, Burton-on-Trent
- Glan Clwyd District General Hospital NHS Trust, Clwyd
- Greenwich Healthcare NHS Trust, London
- Winchester and Eastleigh NHS Trust, Winchester
- The Ipswich Hospital NHS Trust, Ipswich

Short visits were also made to:
- Aintree Hospitals NHS Trust, Liverpool
- Darlington Memorial Hospital NHS Trust, Darlington
- GeneCIS Project, Morriston Hospital NHS Trust, Swansea
- Wrexham Maelor Hospital NHS Trust, Wrexham
- James Paget Hospital NHS Trust, Great Yarmouth
- Preston Acute Hospitals NHS Trust, Preston
- The City Hospital, Sunderland
- Arrowe Park Hospital, Wirral Hospital Trust, Cheshire

Information was also gathered from three pilot audit sites:
- Royal Berkshire Hospitals Trust, Royal Berkshire and Battle Hospitals NHS Trust, Reading
- The City Hospital NHS Trust, Birmingham
- Leicester Royal Infirmary NHS Trust, Leicester

Visits were also made to the following commissioning authorities:
- Bexley & Greenwich Health
- Cambridgeshire and Huntingdon Health Commission
- Clwyd Health Authority
- North and Mid-Hampshire Health Authority
- South Staffordshire Health Authority

Visits were also made to ten GP practices including fundholders.

International visits were made to:

- France — Robert Debre Childrens' Hospital, Paris
  Maçon Hospital, Maçon
- Netherlands — BAZIS Foundation, Leiden
  AZL Leiden University Hospital
  AZR Rotterdam University Hospital
- United States — Veterans Memorial Hospital, Washington
  Moses H. Cone Hospital, Greensboro, North Carolina
  Beth Israel Hospital, Boston, Mass.
  SCAMC Conference, Washington DC
- Switzerland — DIOGENE Project, Geneva University Hospital

Advisory group

The study team was supported by an advisory group consisting of:

- Tim Benson — Managing Director, Abies Consulting
- Alan T Brown — Audit Commissioner
- Dr Richard Gibbs — Chief Executive, Kingston & Richmond Health Authority
- Chris Hurford — Associate Director, Central Computer Audit Unit, Audit Commission
- John R Mason — Director of Medical Services and Consultant Surgeon, Shotley Bridge Hospital, Consett, Co. Durham
- Joe Owens — Chief Executive, Edinburgh Royal Infirmary
- Mike O'Flynn — Director, Information Management Group, NHS Executive
- Victor Peel — Senior Fellow, Health Services Research Management Unit, University of Manchester
- Dr Martin Severs — Consultant Geriatrician, Queen Alexander Hospital, Portsmouth
- Ian Smith — Director of Strategic Planning, Information Management Group, NHS Executive
- Gill Skillicorn — Director of Information, The Ipswich Hospital, Suffolk
- Peter Smith — Director of Finance, Berkshire Health Commission
- Murray Stewart — Deputy Chairman, Audit Commission
- Heather Strachan — Project Manager, Management Development Group, Scottish NHS Management Executive
- Colin Waywell — Chairman, Computer Services Association
- Dr Patricia Wilkie — Vice-Chairman, Patients Association
- Dr David Young — Consultant Physician, The City Hospital NHS Trust, Birmingham

Appendix B

The Audit Commission's report on patient health records

A synopsis of some important findings from the Audit Commission publication on patient health records:

General issues

◆ Hospitals should recognise the value of properly managed information and the benefit it can confer on themselves, their patients and all those involved in caring for the patient.

◆ Hospitals should agree a casenote architecture setting down the optimal content and order of entries in the note.

◆ Clinicians should be required to produce clear statements of key details for summaries (e.g. discharge letters) to assist coders and other re-users of the information (e.g. contract managers), and their performance in this regard should be monitored.

◆ There should be only one record per patient in a hospital.

◆ Wherever possible, there should be only one store for casenotes in each hospital; a system for tracing these casenotes when out of store should be implemented to minimise problems of missing records.

◆ Policies should be implemented whereby the records are culled and weeded to remove unnecessary material, which should be archived or destroyed.

◆ Records should be stored and moved with proper attention to their security, recognising the sensitive nature of their contents.

◆ All staff should be made aware of the need for security (especially confidentiality) of personal information.

◆ Access to patient casenotes should be restricted, limited to those with a legitimate need-to-know.

Specific issues

◆ Multiple records for the same patient (all containing different data items) were found in 75 per cent of hospitals. Care providers keep separate sets of notes because they find it too difficult to find and extract the items of interest to them from the main folder, and/or because the service from the records library is inadequate and leaves them too often without essential records.

◆ Multiple disintegrated records for the same individual lead to a rise in error rates, because clinicians may be unaware of vital information held in one of the sub-records to which they do not have access.

◆ Abstraction of data from records (e.g. by coders for casemix grouping, by clinicians to send to GPs) suffers because data items are 'hidden' and are missed when preparing the abstract; this has a detrimental effect on integrity of care as well as on quality of data in reports sent for activity analysis and contract management.

◆ 36% of casenotes were not immediately available from the record library when required.

◆ 30% of history sheets were inadequate – not legible/dated/timed/signed.

◆ 20% of prescription sheets were illegible.

◆ 40% of handwritten discharge medication sheets were illegible.

◆ 80% of medical records did not have a patient identifier on every piece of paper filed within them; if a piece of paper without an identifier drops out, it may be lost, inserted with the wrong episode or, worse, appended to the wrong set of casenotes.

◆ 40% of records were not well kept or up to date.

◆ 50% of records had no index of contents at the front.

◆ 90% of discharge summaries contained no reference to any information given to the patient or relatives.

Appendix C

An overview of coding and classification

Just as there are many different ways of saying the same thing, so there are many different coding systems each designed for a specific purpose.

A CODE is simply an alternative to the 'plain English' representation of an item, optimised for the use of automated systems. Typically, it is a string of keyboard characters, such as 'Gjo3x' or '310.24'. For any coding system there is a set of valid codes, i.e. codes that are meaningful as opposed to codes that are nonsense, and this can be used to validate (to a limited extent) data entry.

A CLASSIFICATION is a way of grouping together a class of items that share common characteristics and separating them from other items from which they differ significantly. Depending on the purpose of making the classification, different criteria will be used to define a class. There are as many ways of classifying objects as there are purposes for those classifications. Moreover, a classification built for one purpose is generally useful only for that purpose and cannot usefully serve any other purpose.

As an example, consider the classification of fruit. The packagers might classify fruit according to need for transportation and susceptibility to damage (e.g. hard, soft, easy-to-bruise, hard-to-bruise etc.), while the wholesaler might be more concerned with shelf life (e.g. perishes <24 hours, 24-48 hours, >48 hours). The window display dresser would be more interested in colours and ease of stacking and the consumer in eating quality. Medicine has many coding and classification systems, used for recording causes of morbidity and mortality (e.g. ICD9/10, SNOMED), items of service (e.g. OPCS4, CPT4), reasons for encounters (e.g. ICPC, ICHPPC), resource consumption, claims and billing (e.g. DRG, HRG), medications (e.g. BNF), therapeutic agents and appliances, aetiologies of illness (e.g. SNOP) and many more. The number of systems in use continues to grow, since there is a strong urge in the health sector to develop local coding systems where an existing system is felt to be too complex or in some other way inappropriate.

It is unnecessary for those in charge of information in a hospital to know the details of these classifications. But it is vital that they recognise that data collected using one classification will not normally be capable of representation in another. It is only if the raw data items are recorded at the ultimate level of granularity, that is where every individual item is assigned a unique code, that a translation to other classification systems becomes possible. This goal of the Read codes is to enable every individual item of health information to be uniquely coded and to provide a series of standard cross-maps to other classification systems in common usage for specific purposes.

Appendix D

Integrating or interconnecting systems

There are two main approaches to implementing computerised information management systems. One is to procure an integrated system from a single supplier, with different modules to cover specific applications. The other is to interconnect specific applications from a number of different vendors. There are advantages and disadvantages to each (Exhibit A).

Exhibit A
Potential advantages and disadvantages of integrated versus interconnected systems

Advantage	Disadvantage
Integrated	
Data integrity through tightly linked systems	Modules may not be 'best-of-breed'
Common 'look and feel'	Modules may not use new technology
Training in one system only	Often inflexible, difficult and costly to change
System operationally efficient	High costs to tailor to needs of a site
	Centrally driven and often monolithic
	Previous investment in systems a write-off
	Lack of ownership by users
	High initial costs, but may be financed gradually
	Systems costly to maintain and operate
	Specialised skills required to support
Interconnected	
'Best-of-breed' systems used	May present data integration problems
Investment spread over time easier to manage	Likely to be architecturally complicated
Disruption when implementation staged over time	Needs meticulous planning and integration
Can often accommodate existing system investments as servers	Deployment of staff may be restricted by need to re-train them to use different systems
Easier to adapt and grow	
Evolutionary, can respond easily to needs of local users	

References

1. *The evaluation of the Technicon medical information system (at El Camino)*, Medicomp Conference, Berlin 1977.

2. E Drazen, J Metzer, *Methods for Evaluating Costs of Automated Hospital Information System*, NCHSR Research Summary Series, Washington: National Centre of Health Services Research.

3. L H Andersson, *A Computer Aided Medical Information System in a Local Health District in the County Of Uppsula, Sweden*, in Proceedings of the 6th. European Conference on Health Records, Ecomed, 1986: p234-237.

4. NJ Gantz, *The Impact of Information Systems in Critical Care - A Vehicle For Doing More Wth Less Resources*, Medical Informatics Europe, 1990, R O'Moore, S Bengtsson, J R Bryant, J S Bryden (eds), 1990: p182-185.

5. H B J Nieman, *Computerised Nursing Care Plans*, Medical Informatics Europe, 1985, F H Roger, P Gronroos, R Tervo-Pellikka, R O'Moore (eds), 1985: p743-749.

6. JC Wyatt, *Clinical Data Systems*, The Lancet, 1994

7. Audit Commission, *Opportunity Makes A Thief: An Analysis of Computer Abuse*, HMSO, 1994 .

8. Data Protection Act, 1984.

9. *Guidelines on the Protection of Privacy and Trans-border flows of Personal Data*, Paris; OECD, 1981.

10. Council of Europe; *Convention No 108 for the Protection of Individuals with Regard to Automatic Processing of Personal Data*, 28.01.81, Strasbourg:EC 1981.

11. Council of Europe; *Regulations for Automated Medical Data Banks*, Recommendation no R (81) 1 adopted by the Committee of Ministers of the Council of Europe on 23 January 1981, and Explanatory Memorandum, Strasbourg: EC 1981.

12. Computer Misuse Act, 1990.

13. Access to Medical Records Act, 1990.

14. Privacy Act, 1993 and *Code of Practice under the Privacy Act Covering Information held by Health Agencies*.

15. Khan G , *Computer-based Patient Education: A Progress Report*, M D Computing, Vol 10, No2, 1993.

16. Audit Commission, *What Seems to be the Matter*: *Communication Between Hospitals and Patients*, HMSO, 1993.

17. S Greenfield, S Kaplan, JE Ware, *Expanding Patient Involvement in Care: Effects on Patient Outcomes*, Ann Intern Med 1985, 102:520-8.

18. Department of Health, *Patients Charter*, HMSO, April 1992.

19. Association of Community Health Councils for England and Wales, *Did Not Attends (DNAs)*, May 1994.

20. NHS Executive, Information Management Group, *Read Codes and the Terms Projects : a Brief Guide,* February 1995, HMSO.

21. Price Waterhouse, *Information Technology Review,* 1992/93.

22. NHS Management Executive, *An Information and Technology Strategy for the NHS in England,* 1992, HMSO.

23. NHS Management Executive, Information Management Group, Clinical Coding Support Unit, *Data Quality, Patient Classification Systems, and Audit: a Recent Study,* Proceedings of Healthcare 1994 Conference, 1994.

24. 1991 National Confidential Enquiry into Peri-Operative Deaths.

25. Department of Health and Welsh Office, *Hospital Episode Statistics,* 1992/3 and 1993/4.

26. Audit Commission, *Setting the Records Straight: A Study of Hospital Medical Records,* HMSO, 1995.

27. S. Corcoran-Perry and J Graves, *Supplemental Information-Seeking Behaviour of Cardiovascular Nurses,* Research in Nursing & Health, 119-127, 1990.

28. Audit Commission, *Caring Systems: A Handbook for Managers of Nursing and Project Managers,* HMSO, 1992.

29. NHS Management Executive, *Approving IM&T Investment - Further Guidance,* EL(94)22, 1994.

30. NHS Executive, *Priorities and Planning Guidance for the NHS: EL(94)55,* 1995/96.

31. The Nuffield Provincial Hospitals Trust: *A Review of the Current Status and Future Requirements for IT in the NHS,* 1994.

32. Booz Allen Healthcare Inc, J Phillip Lathrop, *Restructuring Health Care -The Patient Focussed Paradigm,* 1994.

33. NHS Executive, *Public Service, Private Finance,* HMSO, 1994.

34. NHS Executive, HSG(94)31, HMSO, 1994.

35. NHS Executive, *Capital Investment Manual,* HMSO, 1994.

36. Greenhalgh & Company Limited, *Nursing Information Systems, Evaluation Report,* 1994.

37. Dorenfast, Charles, Robson and Cohen, *Benefits Realisation and Re-engineering: Essential Tools for a Successful HISS,* Proceedings of Healthcare 1994 Conference, 1994.

38. B Griffin, *Effects of Work Design on Employee Perceptions, Attitudes, and Behaviours: A Long Term Investigation,* Academy of Management Journal, 34, p425-435, 1991.

39. E Gardiner, *Information systems: Computers' Full Capabilities Often Go Untapped,* Modern Healthcare, May 28, p38-40.

40. Dowling, *Do Hospital Staff Interfere with Computer System Implementation?* Health Care Review, 5, P23-32, 1980.

41. NHS Executive, *Draft Guidance for the NHS on Confidentiality, Use and Disclosure of Personal Health Information,* 1994.

42. The Welsh Office, *Draft Guidance for the NHS on Confidentiality, Use and Disclosure of Personal Health Information,* 1994.

Index References are to paragraph numbers